music of the classic period

The Brown Music Horizons Series

Books now available

MUSIC IN THE UNITED STATES—*Arthur C. Edwards and W. Thomas Marrocco*, U.C.L.A.

MUSIC THROUGH THE RENAISSANCE—*James C. Thomson*, University of Kansas

THE CONCERTO—*Wendell Nelson*, University of California

MUSIC OF THE ROMANTIC PERIOD—*Johannes Riedel*, University of Minnesota

MUSIC OF THE CLASSIC PERIOD—*Theodore E. Heger*, University of Michigan

music of the classic period

Theodore E. Heger
University of Michigan

WM. C. BROWN COMPANY PUBLISHERS, *Dubuque, Iowa*

MUSIC SERIES

Consulting Editor
  Frederick W. Westphal
  Sacramento State College

Copyright © 1969 by
Wm. C. Brown Company Publishers

Library of Congress Catalog Card Number: 69-16170

ISBN 0–697–03403–8

Second Printing, 1970

Printed in the United States of America

The tremendous growth and interest in basic music appreciation and literature courses and the increasing emphasis on music for the general college student demands fresh approaches to teaching and learning at the introductory level.

The Music Horizons Series represents a significant attempt to meet these needs by providing students with stimulating material of high quality by an authority in the field as well as providing instructors with the advantage of complete flexibility in organizing and teaching their course. Although the individual titles are self-contained, collectively they cover the full scope of music appreciation, literature and history.

preface

The music of the eighteenth century has been of particular interest to scholars and laymen alike in the twentieth century. Somehow they seem to sense a closer affinity to that period than they do to the neighboring nineteenth century. Whereas the composer of the Romantic era displayed an almost unbridled emotion in his music and aimed to move his audience to sympathetic feeling, the contemporary composer looks with disdain upon such out-and-out exhibitionism. It is true that in keeping with the social code of the day, eighteenth-century artists suppressed their emotions or at least kept them under control, but it is fallacious to assume that they were devoid of feeling or approached their art in the light of cold intellect as many believe today.

The contemporary composer is likely to be concerned largely with developing his craftsmanship and in experimentation. By the time we reach the Classic era, on the other hand, forms in music and orchestral balance and instrumentation had been well established. It is a period which promotes such media as concertos and sonatas to exploit the virtuosity of performers; of operatic arias to challenge the skill of the singer. Like the modern composer, the eighteenth-century composer had to justify his art in the light of science, for the Classic period too was an age which glorified scientific achievement.

This book is intended to be informative to those who have a limited knowledge of music. Obviously it is not meant to be an all-embracing treatise on the music of the eighteenth century nor does it dwell at length on harmonic and formal analysis. What is intended is a lucid presentation of factual material which might serve as a springboard to further study and listening. It should help clarify the reader's thinking, to aid him in understanding better the vast amount of literature from this period which even today goes to make up such a considerable portion of our concert and recital repertoire.

A glance at the table of contents will indicate that the approach taken is one which considers the music by medium of expression. Although composers in the eighteenth century were versatile and wrote for many media, this book, by categorizing these media and by so treating the material, fulfills its objective to make clear the approach to further study.

It must be kept in mind that music is an art of sound, and accumulating knowledge about the music of the Classic era is no substitute for listening and getting to know some of the great masterpieces of this fascinating period.

Theodore E. Heger

*compare 2 forms
& 2 composers
those forms*

☀ what is classicism ?

contents

Mozart's Requiem

background of the eighteenth century

INTRODUCTION

History shows us that each generation condemns the previous generation for one fault or another. So too does each century look upon the last as the least desirable in which to live, its philosophy at opposite poles from its own. Critics, philosophers, historians, and artists of the nineteenth century damned the eighteenth century as the "Age of Prose and Reason"—rationalistic, shallow, narrow in its outlook, with a culture that was at best static. Our own generation has come to look on the eighteenth century with far less prejudice.

The eighteenth century was a crossroads of dozens of tendencies in music, some beginning in the seventeenth century and ending in the nineteenth century. It saw the beginnings of a system of harmony with which we are most familiar, the kind we associate with the music of Bach and Handel, with Haydn and Mozart. This is often referred to as "functional" harmony. It saw also the crystallization and codification of forms and styles that serve as the backbone of a vast literature out of which our concert and recital repertoire is made.

Like our own twentieth century, particularly after the launching of Sputnik I, the eighteenth century found art on the defensive in a scientific age. Art had to justify itself in the light of science. It was also a period that looked with disdain upon any open display of emotions, even upon art. But paradoxically the forces which tended to destroy music seemed to provide fertile ground for it to develop.

Viewed from our vantage point, the eighteenth century seems such a stable, balanced, and even age. Yet one of the chief characteristics of the century was the fact that it was a period of conflict. We have, for example, despotism vs. democracy or absolutism vs. enlightenment, a conflict which grew out of the rising demand for equal rights and universal education against the privileges which had been enjoyed only by the wealthy class. With the coming Industrial Revolution a conflict ensued between agriculture and industry. In the area of philosophy there was a conflict between rationalism (absolute thinking) and empiricism (absolute experience). The empiricists, accepting the principles of Francis Bacon, Locke, and Diderot, claimed that experience was the basis of all knowledge, while the rationalistic scientists, following the footsteps of Descartes and Newton, used mathematical measurements to explain all phenomena. There is no truth, said the Enlightenment, which cannot stand the test of reason. There arose also a conflict between science and religion. Philosophers no longer believed in miracles, and if they believed in God at all, they considered Him a kind of cosmic mechanic who had built a marvelous machine, given it a law on which it could operate, and then withdrawn. So, they thought, the only reliable road to knowledge of God's plans was through science, not religion, through observation and experiment, not through dogma and revolution. The eighteenth century emerged from authority, especially church authority, to freedom of thought. There is also the conflict of Classicism and Romanticism. We are liable to put the label of Classicism on the whole of the eighteenth century, but we forget that it was also the cradle of Romanticism with occasional outbursts that are reflected in art, especially in music.

A second characteristic is that of balance. One reads dissertations on political balance of power in which no country shall become stronger than another. This idea prevails even in our own time with respect to political ideologies, and the principle of balance is reflected in literature and music. The rhyming couplet of Alexander Pope exemplifies this. In his *Essay on Criticism* he speaks of universal knowledge with:

> True wit is nature to advantage dress'd
> What oft was thought, but ne'er so well express'd.

There is generally a pause at the end of each line, and each couplet, when detached from the context, will usually make complete sense. Not only in poetry but in prose as well is this balance seen. The style of essay writing was to construct sentences with dependent and independent clauses, one balancing the other. Here is a typical sentence taken from Lord Chesterfield's *Letters* to his son, dated November 20, 1739:

As you are now reading the Roman History,
I hope you do it with that care and attention which it deserves.
The utility of History consists principally in the examples it gives us
      of virtues and vices of those who have gone before us;
upon which we ought to make the proper observations.

In music we get the same kind of balance. There are often two phrases, an antecedent and a consequent which complement each other, as is shown in the opening theme of Mozart's Quartet in G minor for Piano and Strings (K.478):

Mozart: Quartet in G minor for Piano and Strings (K. 478)., 1st movement

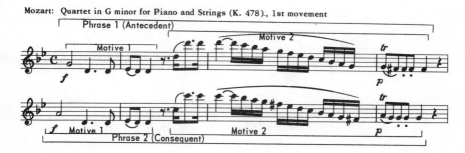

The eighteenth century was a cosmopolitan age. Not only did foreign-born kings rule countries such as England, Poland, Russia, and others, but foreign-born musicians, especially Italian, abounded in countries other than their own. England was subject to an invasion of Italian artists and composers as were Germany and Russia. German symphonists invaded France. A universal musical style prevailed emanating largely from Italy, for that country was the mecca for musicians all over the world. Composers like Handel, Hasse, and Mozart were trained in the Italian style. However, other countries such as Germany and France made contributions to this universal style so that the eighteenth century is an amalgamation of features stemming from several countries but blended into a homogeneous whole.

It was an age of clarity. The second generation of composers practiced a style called "homophonic" in which a clearly-defined theme is but slightly accompanied with a simple harmonic structure that never detracts from the melody. Polyphony was frowned upon, for it implied confusion. "How can one hear two or more different melodies going on at the same time?" was a question often posed. Art, like science, had to exist in clear, lucid, distinct ideas, unclouded by passion and imagination. Sir John Denham (1615-1669), an English poet, in a poem celebrating the Thames River, prophetically summed up the classic, eighteenth-century attitude as follows:

> Oh, could I flow like thee, and make thy stream
> My great example, as it were, my theme,
> Thou deep, yet clear; thou gentle, yet not dull;
> Strong without rage
> Without o'erflowing full.

Paradoxically the eighteenth century sought new ideas and yet was apprehensive of them. It wanted to be thought in the new mode yet clung desperately to the old and outmoded. It was the meeting place of dozens of tendencies. Haydn climaxed the ideas of C.P.E. Bach, and Beethoven departed on independent paths, just as Pope continued the tradition of Dryden, and Wordsworth broke away from the fetters imposed upon these men. Haydn, Beethoven, Pope, and Wordsworth all belong to the eighteenth century but to different ends of it. One or the other saw the beginning, the fruition, and the end of infinite streams of varied expression.

To the eighteenth century, music aimed at being entertaining. Its language had to be free of complexities and make an immediate appeal to the normal listener. Like the medium of English watercolor in art so popular at the time, music generally involved happiness: it could record mood but rarely passion; it tended to charm rather than arouse. And its sound and style were to be universal, unimpeded by national idiosyncrasies.

DIVISIONS OF TIME AND ARTISTIC TRENDS IN THE EIGHTEENTH CENTURY

Despite the artificiality of the procedure and the perils inherent in oversimplification, the most convenient method of approaching the stylistic features of the eighteenth century is to divide the era into three generations of composers. The first period, from 1700 to about 1730, may be designated as the late Baroque; the second, from about 1730 to 1770, the Rococo; and the third, from 1770 to about the second decade of the nineteenth century, the Classic. These terms, Baroque, Rococo, Classic, borrowed from art history, are in themselves, as far as music is concerned, oftentimes misleading or meaningless. But they serve as convenient tags or labels. Too frequently the art of the eighteenth century is contemplated as if it were a single, homogeneous block of airy and delicate music. This is a completely false assumption. Each generation had a different objective and created a new stylistic trend.

Let us go back a short distance in time to see how events led to the kind of music we can expect to find in the eighteenth century. When the Renaissance reached its climax in the sixteenth century, a powerful spiritual fermentation was precipitated which became known as the Protestant Reformation. At first ignored by the Catholic Church as another annoying heretical uprising, the Church soon came to realize that it was dealing with a deep-seated rebellion which called for counter measures. Among the measures used to prevent the further spread of Protestantism was the device of propaganda, and it soon permeated arts and letters. Architects, painters, and musicians began to create works on a gigantic scale to overwhelm the populace. Art in the form of huge murals, architecture with immense buildings and colonnades, and musical compositions engaging the services of a multitude of performers to produce voluminous sound are part and parcel of a movement that is called the Counter-Reformation.

A similar situation, but on a smaller scale, occurred in the twentieth century when television sets became practical for every household to acquire. People abandoned the cinema houses to concentrate their attention on the little square box in their homes. The motion picture industry responded with a wider and wider screen and stereophonic sound that emanated from all directions. Advertised as "living presence" the industry began to lure television addicts back to the theaters.

The beginning of the seventeenth century saw the Counter-Reformation at its height, and while it had been initiated by the Roman Church, features of the Counter-Reformation were appropriated by the Protestant North as well. In the course of the century these excesses calmed down, and a majestic, solidly-constructed style permeated art. This is best revealed in the music of Johann Sebastian Bach (1685-1750) and Georg Friedrich Handel (1685-1759).

The Baroque Generation

The Baroque style in music involves two textures: the *amphonic* and the *polyphonic* or a combination of both. The amphonic (from the Greek, *amphi*, "on both sides," and *phōné*, "sound") style implies a clearly-defined melody supported by an active bass. With the rise of monody at the beginning of the seventeenth century the top melody came into new prominence along with the soloist who performed it. But peculiarly the bass line in the Baroque also assumed a leading role. It usually moves continuously (hence the term *basso continuo*) and gives rise to frequent changes of harmony which we refer to as rapid harmonic rhythm. Here is an example:

Purcell: Dido and Aeneas

The inner parts are of no great concern to either the composer or the listener; indeed the composer did not even bother to write out the harmony on a keyboard part used to accompany a soloist or ensemble. By means of numbers placed below the bass notes the composer directed the organist or harpsichordist (the harpsichord in the seventeenth and through most of the eighteenth century was the principal keyboard instrument) as to what harmonies should be played in the right hand.

Bach: St. Matthew Passion

This shorthand system saved the composer considerable time since he did not have to write out all the notes of the keyboard part. The burden was placed on the performer and his skill in interpreting the figured bass (or "thorough-bass"). Hence no two performances might ever be identical either by different players or even by the same keyboard artist. Because the bass line was so important and because the harpsichord had a relatively small tone, the bass was reinforced. Hence in a violin sonata, for example, it was not enough that a harpsichord provide the accompaniment, but the bass would be emphasized by the addition of a low-stringed instrument, such as a cello, duplicating the bass being played in the harpsichord.

The second style found in the Baroque is polyphony. It is a complex texture in which each part (soprano, alto, tenor, bass) has an independent melodic line which when combined with the other parts produces a web of sound that in Bach's time follows some harmonic plan. Polyphony may result from successive imitation of voices as in a fugue or simply combine different streams of melody. The history of music from about 1000 to 1600 is concerned largely with the evolution and development of polyphonic techniques. At the beginning of the seventeenth century composers abandoned polyphony to devote their attention to the amphonic style. However, it was not long before they realized that polyphony is or at least polyphonic devices are a necessary adjunct to compositional procedure. So toward the end of the seventeenth century and on into the first generation of the eighteenth century, polyphony along with amphony is an important stylistic feature of music. Indeed the two styles are often combined as in the Credo movement from Bach's B minor Mass in which the active instrumental bass supports a harmonic structure over which a complex fugal texture is carried on by the voices.

It was this first generation of composers in the eighteenth century that established the harmonic system with which we are best acquainted. Rules of chord progression were established and followed by men like Jean-Philippe Rameau (1683-1764) and practiced almost universally. Out of the relationship of chords came the modern major and minor modes.

Another significant factor in characterizing the Baroque is the emphasis on contrasting effects, called *stile concertante*. These contrasts included such marked differences as loud and soft. The seventeenth century did not indicate on its scores varied shades of intensity, only *forte* (loud) and *piano* (soft). A whole movement of a sonata might be played loud followed by a movement played soft, or a single passage might be played loud followed by a repetition of that passage played soft, thus creating a kind of echo effect. Or in chamber music a large body of instruments could initiate a thematic idea to be followed by a solo instrument with perhaps an accompaniment of a harpsichord repeating the idea. Even though both the ensemble and soloist would play *forte*, the effect of two bodies of players would create a timbre producing the desired contrast. Contrast was also obtained by tempo, a fast movement followed by a slow movement, or the reverse. Meter too serves as contrast. A movement might be in triple rhythm followed by one in duple meter. Last there is the contrast of texture. A movement or passage in chordal style could be followed by one in polyphonic style. Contrast lies at the very root of Baroque philosophy.

The period is also noteworthy for its elaborate ornamentation. Art works—painting and sculpture—and architecture fairly crawl with elaborate decoration. So too is the melodic line of solo musical compositions. A melody appearing in a composer's manuscript or on the printed copy looks so simple and straight-forward, often consisting of a succession of quarter notes not unlike that found in a chorale in a hymnal. However, the performer was expected to improvise ornaments so that the melody of simple quarter notes would become an elaborate coloratura. French composers like François Couperin (1668-1733) often indicated with special symbols the ornaments they wished executed. The Germans and more particularly the Italians were rather negligent in writing them down, leaving the ornamentation to the judgment of the performer. Singers especially, in the seventeenth and eighteenth centuries, who had reached a height of virtuosity never surpassed, took delight in opera arias in elaborating on the printed melody. But it must be kept in mind that instrumentalists as well—violinists, flutists, and oboists— practiced this art of improvisation. Indeed improvisation is an important aspect of the Baroque. Even poets in European courts were expected to create rhyming verses on the spot like the modern calypso singer. The harpsichordist when "realizing" the harmony above a figured bass as has been described was in a sense improvising.

The Baroque liked voluminous sound. Cardinal Benedetto Panphilij's orchestra, which Corelli conducted in Rome, consisted of 39 violins, 10 violas, 17 violoncellos, 10 double basses, one lute, and 2 trumpets. At San Petronio in Bologna the roster of musicians employed for ordinary Sunday services ran from 30 to 50 players. There is further evidence that orchestras on feast days numbered anywhere from 150 to 200 players. Only in England did they consider several persons to a part as awkward and vulgar.

Melody in Baroque music may be motivic, that is, it may consist of a figure or figures which, when repeated either on the same level or on different tonal levels, allows for an expansion of a musical idea:

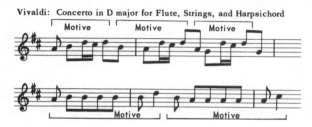

Vivaldi: Concerto in D major for Flute, Strings, and Harpsichord

Or we may have a long-breathed melody without rests and without the repetition of musical figures. It seems to spin out from an initial idea, moving continuously. Although the concept of the four-measure phrase of melody balanced by another four-measure phrase in art music other than the dance has its start early in the eighteenth century, it will take the succeeding generations of the century to establish this as a norm. One rather strange phenomenon, and we find it in instrumental ensemble music, is the sometimes complete lack of melody. The music consists largely of harmonic progressions. Confronted with the problem of writing music without a text to stimulate their imaginations, composers may have been at this time at a loss as to how to proceed. We are not speaking here of the fugue but only of those forms which have no prescribed formulae. It is an interesting speculation.

What has been said of Baroque music can be applied to painting. If we look at the reproduction here of Rembrandt's *Staalmeesters,* or *Syndics of the Cloth Guild* (1661-62), we will see how like a polyphonic composition it is. The theme is a meeting of the guild. Although each figure shows distinct personality, each is necessary to the com-

pletely communal spirit of the group, like the melodic lines of a polyphonic texture adhering to a basic harmony. Rembrandt achieved this
unity within diversity by capturing a moment in which one syndic has
just finished speaking, while another, half rising from his chair, turns
as though to address the audience. The two men farthest left and the
pair at the right look directly at the beholder, creating absolute balance.
The servant standing behind looks in the same direction as the central
syndic. Color contrast is suggested by the soft golden light falling over
the windows at the left. This relieves the sobriety of the black-garbed
individuals and the severe paneling of the room.

The Rococo Generation

But while Bach was working on his masterpieces of polyphonic
grandeur, a new style came to the fore, the Rococo. A new generation
of composers, and Bach's sons belong to this generation, looked askance
at the products of their forebears, the mighty Handelian oratorio, the
Passions and fugues of Bach. The Rococo, or *style galant*, originated in
France during the reigns of Louis XIV and Louis XV and spread to
the rest of Europe. Suites of dances replaced preludes and fugues;
shallow sentimental pieces replaced the great choral works.

The social life of the period of which music is a reflection reveals
an affinity for trivialities and intimate salon gatherings. This world of
sophisticated charm, grace, and gallant manners was perfectly represented in Watteau's idyllic paintings of nymphs and shepherds and the
gay upper-class life of the day. It was also reflected in the whole over-
throw of Baroque grandeur and monumentality on the part of eighteenth-
century artists. Splendor was replaced by polished elegance and minute,
delicate decoration. It was as if the gilt were now being applied with
a finer brush capable of more detail.

Everyone, it seems, had a passion for beautiful art objects during
this period, and the arts flourished in a manner not unlike that of the
Renaissance. Kings subsidized silversmiths, and the large and prosperous
middle class provided the audience and the market for artists and
composers. The middle class exerted a powerful influence on artistic
creation in that it now appeared as subjects in works of art and in
literature. Artists moved out of the mythological past into the very real
present. The increased number of opera houses built and the rise of
the public concert attest to the rise in importance of the bourgeois.

The second generation of composers felt that Baroque music was
too massive and difficult to comprehend. Bach's sons looked upon their
father's complex counterpoint as unapproachable. They believed, like

others of their generation, that music was meant to gratify the senses, not tax the intellect. To their generation polyphony was anathema. There arose a style in which there is a clearly-defined theme in the upper part with a slight harmonic accompaniment. How does this differ from the amphonic style? Whereas the amphonic had an active bass that implied frequent harmonic changes, the new style—called the *homophonic*—had a lazy-moving bass pivoting largely on the primary notes of the scale: I, IV, and V. Thus the harmony, still improvised on the harpsichord by the figured-bass system, was extremely simple with frequent repetitions of the same chord in what is called slow harmonic rhythm, losing the interesting character it had had in the Baroque.

In the usual Baroque texture, a motive was generally imitated and manipulated throughout a piece, and the music proceeded steadily without interruption. When in the Rococo period imitation was abandoned as the most important musical procedure, the continuous musical flow was broken up into definite, symmetrical phrases by cadences. But these short motives with their usual jagged melodic patterns so well suited to imitative treatment could not stand alone as the main thread in the music as conceived by Rococo composers. So a longer, smoother, and instantly recognizable melody replaced the Baroque motive. This we call a theme, and it was to rule music for several succeeding generations. The Baroque motive or subject gained significance only in its contrapuntal treatment. The new theme was independent and could stand by itself as a musical entity. The Rococo composer simplified music for the listener by giving him guide-posts to follow such as themes and cadences.

From architectural massiveness we move to mere playful prettiness. The new generation had a penchant for solo instrumentation. This is the era that saw the rise of the solo sonata and concerto in instrumental music. The accompaniment of the operatic aria did not interfere with the voice part. It is unfortunately a rather low point in the quality of musical endeavor in the eighteenth century.

There are really two movements going on simultaneously in the Rococo period: (1) the evolutionary and (2) the revolutionary. The evolutionary forces freed themselves from the theatricality, profundity, and academicism of the Baroque without withdrawing from the courtly, aristocratic atmosphere in which the Baroque had flourished. There is a hovering lightness about the profuse ornamentation to be found in all art. This can best be illustrated with a painting of Jean Antoine Watteau entitled *Embarkation for Cythera* (1717) which depicts the beginning of the voyage of lovers to an island paradise. Here Watteau has pic-

Rembrandt van Rijn: **Staalmeesters,** or **Syndics of the Cloth Guild**
(1661/2). Amsterdam: Rijks Museum. (Courtesy, Art Reference Bureau.)

Jean Antione Watteau: **Embarkation for Cythera** (1717). Berlin: Royal
Palace. (Courtesy, Art Reference Bureau.)

tured the aristocracy in its silks and satins set in a charming landscape decorated with a profusion of cupids like the graces that adorn the melodies of Rococo music.

The clavecin (French for harpsichord) compositions of François Couperin yield the best examples of the styles we have described. There is an air of elegance about them, the austerity of the Baroque theme has yielded to a melody extravagant with ornamentation, and the rich harmony has yielded to limpid, broken chords. Couperin's are short, witty pieces, each sustaining a single mood. Many bear programmatic titles.

The revolutionary forces, on the other hand, put an end to the Baroque and led to the period we call the Classic. Human warmth replaced academicism, simplicity replaced pompousness, real life against a sham world, democracy against aristocracy.

The spokesman for the revolutionary was Jean Jacques Rousseau (1712-1778) who had a deep scorn for the artificial society that had grown up during the Enlightenment. His "back-to-nature" philosophy (more properly, back to the natural), his belief that civilization is evil and that man is inherently good until society corrupts him, fascinated eighteenth-century society. Under the influence of his novels (*Émile* and *La Nouvelle Héloise*) the sophisticated people of a highly sophisticated era tried to cultivate simplicity and tenderness, but that society became even more artificial when the nobility donned shepherds' costumes and lived in made-to-order rustic palaces.

All this struggle for the natural inevitably produced secondary currents: simplicity, bourgeois spirit, emotionalism, belittlement of craft. The last mentioned pointed up the important role played by the amateur. Germany's musical production depended to a great extent on laymen. Most German orchestras and choruses of the eighteenth century were *Liebhaberorchester* and *Akademien* of amateurs. With the growing number of enthusiastic amateurs it was necessary to provide them with music they could perform without too great a strain on their technical ability and music whose content they could easily grasp.

Where the evolutionary style was profuse in its use of ornamentation, the revolutionary style dropped most of the graces. Out of the revolutionary movement came the comic opera with its apparent simplicity and sudden changes of mood. Its composers hated pathetic gesture and posing, so prevalent in serious opera. As an example of the revolutionary style the opening aria from Rousseau's comic opera, *Le Devin du Village* (The Village Soothsayer), serves well to illustrate the simple, unadorned treatment of the music.

Rousseau: Le Devin du Village

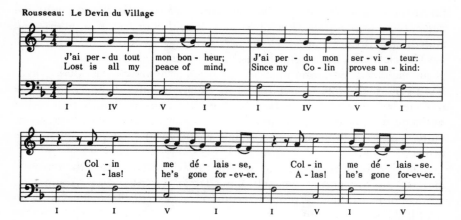

J'ai per - du tout | mon bon - heur; | J'ai per - du mon | ser - vi - teur:
Lost is all my | peace of mind, | Since my Co - lin | proves un - kind:

I   IV   V   I   I   IV   V   I

Col - in | me dé - lais - se, | Col - in | me dé - lais - se.
A - las! | he's gone for - ev - er. | A - las! | he's gone for-ev-er.

I   I   V   I   I   V   I   V

The Classic Generation

Shortly after the middle of the eighteenth century a new spirit began to permeate the arts. We call this spirit Classicism. The stimulus for the movement came from the systematic excavations in 1763 of Herculaneum and Pompeii, Roman cities buried under lava from the eruption of Mt. Vesuvius in A.D. 79. Indeed the search for relics in these buried cities so enthralled the eighteenth century that in England and in Vienna, to name two places, modern ruins were constructed in imitation of the ancient, surviving remains of fallen and decayed buildings. In turning to models of the classical art of ancient Greece and Rome for inspiration, artists were not only enticed by their universal appeal, but they found in them the good taste and perfection of form and reason which they so admired. Classical architecture and poetry were dignified, balanced, symmetrical, and simple.

Architects now concerned themselves with line and structure in opposition to the excessive decoration of the interior which had been such a prominent feature of the Baroque and Rococo. The Elector of Bavaria in 1770 decreed that all ecclesiastical building should be kept simple and noble "with all superfluous stucco-work and other meaningless and ridiculous ornaments" done away with. This aim for simplicity and the stimulation of ancient Roman culture can be observed in the paintings of Jacques Louis David. In his *Oath of the Horatii* (1784) we have a perfect dramatic presentation of ancient Roman heroism set in an appropriate archaeological frame. Abandoned are the subjects depicting royalty disguised as shepherds and shepherdesses. This composition is academic and classic in its simplicity, the figures are sculptured and obviously posed, the color is cool and intellectual, and it is balanced. The room in which the action takes place is square, with three arches in the rear. The center arch frames Brutus; the left, his sons; and the right, their womenfolk. A point to be observed is the strange, individual power of expression that allows each group to stand by itself, yet each takes its place as part of a whole.

The changing attitudes of this new generation are reflected also in the music of the period. Significantly instrumental music emerged as a serious competitor of vocal music. Through most of the course of the eighteenth century, especially in France, aestheticians posed the question, "How can one have a meaningful music without the support of words?" Composers of instrumental music from the period of the Baroque aimed to create a tonal language that could reflect moods and passions—in their mildest forms to be sure. The composers of the Classic era chose to express their ideas within certain disciplined musical forms such as the sonata. Yet such seemingly strict forms allowed the utmost liberty for their imaginations. They considered the sonata-form less of an arbitrary design and more of a compositional procedure. The Baroque and Rococo composers sustained a single mood in the course of a movement for instruments just as they did in an opera aria. The Classic composers are likely to set up a conflict of emotions within a movement or aria and even within a single theme, as we shall see.

Composers of the Classic period were not only masters of musical design and tasteful ornamentation, but they balanced homophony and polyphony in a judicious mixture that for them solved many musical problems. The Rococo had condemned counterpoint much as the early seventeenth century had, and, like the early Baroque, the Classic period soon discovered it could not abandon polyphonic devices. What happened then in musical style was the inclusion of counterpoint in an essentially homophonic style. However the counterpoint is not the strict fugal manipulation of a definite number of real voices as we find in the age of Bach and Handel nor is it the transparent homophony of the Rococo. What the Classic composer did was to develop a style which inwardly united elements of the *style galant* (the term associated with the homophonic style of the Rococo) and the "learned" (the term associated with the contrapuntal style of the Baroque). Here is a sample:

Mozart: Symphony No. 38 in D major ("Prague"), Second Movement

First Violin

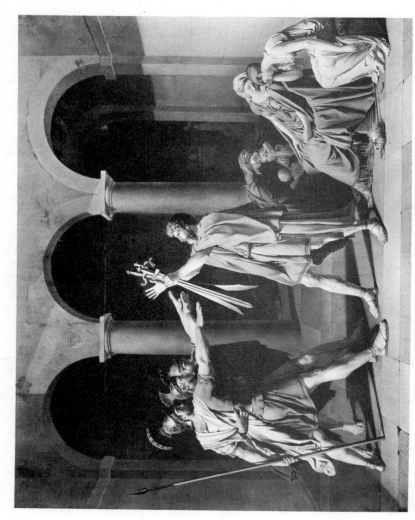

Jacques Louis David: **The Oath of the Horatii.** The Toledo Museum of Art, Toledo, Ohio. Gift of Edward Drummond Libbey, 1950

Counterpoint in the Classic period was used largely as a device of thematic development. It is used to broaden dimensions in phrases and sections. Let us examine the following:

Haydn: Symphony No. 15 in D major, Third Movement: Andante
Here is the basic motive:

Now Haydn combines various forms of the motive to create a theme:

In motives *a b c* the direction of the melody is changed.
In motive *d* both the melody and rhythm are changed.
Then in the development we have the grouping of the motives thus:

Indeed after long study one comes to the conclusion that it is the theme itself that distinguishes the Classic from every other period. By and large the typical theme is motivic. It contains the latent possibilities of fragmentation and development as we have observed in the above example. In addition many of these themes are dual motives. There is nothing new in the use of two motives to form a theme. But what is new is the contrast of mood which often separates these motives yet welds them into a single theme. One can be a powerful unison motive followed by a delicate motive to form a phrase:

Theme — motivic

Mozart: Symphony No. 41 in C major ("Jupiter"), First Movement

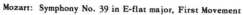
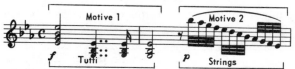

Or the opening motive can be a solid block of chords followed by a soft, scale-like passage:

Mozart: Symphony No. 39 in E-flat major, First Movement

These heterogeneous features within the theme create energy which, when set free, give rise to a conflict that is exploited and then resolved. By dissecting the themes and working them through the fabric of the composition polyphonically we have one of the most important aspects of Classic style.

With respect to ornamentation the Classic period is more tasteful and somewhat more modest in its use of embellishments. And whereas the Baroque and Rococo performers improvised their embellishments, one is more likely to find, in the Classic era, that the composer writes the desired ornamentation into the score so that it becomes an integral part of his conception. To add in performance to what the composer already indicated would be an encroachment on his prerogatives.

Between the Rococo and Classic periods there appeared in the 1770's a short-lived movement in Germany known as the *Sturm und Drang* (storm and stress), named after a drama by Maximilian von Klinger (1776). It was basically a literary movement in which the younger generation of German poets strove for independence against the traditional standards and rigid formalism emanating from France. In content too this movement rebelled against the tasteless optimism existing in eighteenth-century literature that disguised the miseries of life and social wrongs. Goethe and Schiller were the leaders of the *Sturm und Drang,* and they held up as their models Shakespeare and Rousseau. The new emotionalism exhibited passion, vigor, and an individuality unique for the century. But the initial extravagant impulses soon burned themselves out, and Goethe and Schiller sought a calmer expression in the prevailing Classic style. Nevertheless this movement had its impact not only on literature but on painting and music as well. Composers like

C.P.E. Bach and Joseph Haydn translated the feeling to their music. It is interesting to speculate how, if the *Sturm und Drang* had continued as a normal revolutionary movement, Romanticism in the arts would have dawned far earlier than the nineteenth century. As it is, the *Sturm und Drang* remains a unique decade in the eighteenth century with significant overtones.

The three generations of composers which constitute the century, the Baroque, the Rococo, and the Classic, each brought a distinct style and texture to music. The Baroque was concerned with a majestic and massive architectural style utilizing learned counterpoint and amphonic texture. But even while Bach was working on his greatest polyphonic masterpieces, as we have mentioned, his own sons were already under the influence of the new style, the Rococo, with its decorative, homophonic texture. It was a style anathema to the gigantic proportions of Bach's fugues and the impassioned dramatic force of the Handelian oratorio. It brought simplicity and a certain naturalism to the art of music. Then came the Classic generation with its penchant for balance, poise, and dignity. To the homophonic style in secular music were superimposed polyphonic devices which had lain dormant since the Baroque and which during the Rococo had been used only in sacred musical compositions. Somehow polyphony was always associated with church music. Now it becomes an integral part of the basically homophonic texture.

Again it should be emphasized that these divisions are artificial and serve only as a pedagogical means to clearer understanding. Bach and Handel lived and wrote in a time beyond what we have indicated as the close of the Baroque era. Likewise many composers living in the Classical period were still writing in the *style galant*.

This book will deal only with the Rococo and Classic periods. It is organized on the basis of medium—opera, instrumental music, chamber music, sacred music—and stylistic trends.

SUPPLEMENTARY READING

Grout, Donald Jay. *A History of Western Music.* pp. 411-416.
Láng, Paul Henry. *Music in Western Civilization.* pp. 530-543; 567-579; 585-591; 618-625.

opera

SERIOUS OPERA

Music in the eighteenth century was expressed through many media—sonatas, concertos, symphonies, to name a few—but none more important than opera. Opera was the nerve center of music whose features pervaded every aspect of the art, sacred and secular.

At the beginning of the century the serious opera emanating from Italy, and especially Naples, was the universal type which permeated all of Europe except France. Under the influence of two poets, Apostolo Zeno (1668-1750) and Pietro Metastasio (1698-1782), a kind of stereotyped plan was evolved. The plots were based on legends of antiquity or on episodes from medieval and oriental history. All operas, no matter how tragic the circumstances, had to have a happy ending, in which the principal characters—five, six, or seven singers—paired off into two or three happy couples. Regardless of the story there was always a noble hero, an unhappy heroine, and an encroaching villain. There were generally three acts divided into several scenes. A scene could be determined by the entrance of a new character, much as we find it in Shakespeare, or by the musical structure of a single recitative and aria. From opera's very start in 1600 a certain style had been delegated to treat dramatic action and a different style used to represent the protagonist's reaction to the situation. By the close of the seventeenth century the distinction between the two styles grew markedly. That area which dealt with the enfolding of the plot was called a recitative. Generally it was rather free rhythmically and formally and was accompanied only on the harpsichord. That section which was an expression of emotion evoked by the situation was called the aria, and it was written in a recognizable musical design, most frequently three-part (represented by the symbols A B A, A = a musical statement, B = a digression, and A = the return of the first statement).

Occupying the central position as a musical unit, each aria preserved a unity of mood. This is important in the light of later eighteenth-century development of the aria. The poetry of the text was usually built on two stanzas of four lines each. Following is the text of an aria in Handel's masque entitled *Acis and Galatea* (1719):

> A   Love sounds the alarm,
> and fear is a-flying,
> When beauty's the prize,
> What mortal fears dying?
>
> B   In defense of my treasure
> I'd bleed at each vein,
> Without her no pleasure,
> For life is a pain.
>
> A   Love sounds the alarm, etc.

The text served as a springboard for a musical design. Because the words were few and quickly exhausted in the progress of the aria, it was necessary for the composer to repeat phrases and words of the text over and over to fulfill the demands of a musical design. As with the Handel selection the composer first stated the whole text of the initial stanza and then went back to repeat the text in a kind of musical development before proceeding to the next stanza. In Handel this mid-section or B area is shorter than the A section with little repetition of text. It furnishes a brief respite from the material of A. Then the A section returns intact, but with this difference: the singer was obliged to ornament the melodic line, inserting trills and other roulades. It was with this decoration that the vocalist demonstrated his virtuosity. Where an examination of the score itself reveals only a simple melodic line, it was expected that the performer would add embellishments in all the sections but reserving the most elaborate for the final one. The author discovered in the National Library in Vienna a collection of arias dated 1733 written by Farinelli (Carlo Broschi, 1705-1782), perhaps the most famous castrato (artificial male soprano) of all times. In these arias Farinelli's copyist placed the notation of the A section in black ink and the altered line of the *da capo* in red. Here is an example:

Written part

Suggested ornamentation on da capo

The number and order of the arias were strictly regulated. Generally every character was to have at least one aria in each act, but no one might have two arias in succession. The subordinate roles must have fewer and less important arias than the stars, the greatest number being given to the *prima donna* (leading lady) and the *primo uomo* (leading man). It was possible to change the order of the arias, add or omit others, which only goes to prove that an opera was largely a vocal concert in costume. Almost every opera house had its own staff of singers, instrumentalists, and composers. Thus a composer, in writing an opera, had in mind the potentialities and limitations of the singers for whom he wrote. If an opera written for one company was performed by another, the composer of the latter house felt free to insert arias of his own invention. After all there were no copyright laws. Such changes in the original score were called *pasticcio.*

As has been mentioned before, the recitative was usually accompanied only by the harpsichord, the standard keyboard instrument of the period. However, in a few important places in the drama the recitative was accompanied by the orchestra, usually strings. But the audience was seldom interested in this aspect of the opera. It focused its attention only on the arias and the virtuosity of the singers. There was little or no use of a chorus. Perhaps in a finale a body of warriors might declaim, "Hail to the king!" or a similar expression. There were few ensemble numbers, the duet being the most frequent.

Through the aria, singers and composers were devoted to the pure musical beauty of melody and the singing voice. The male singers were generally castrati, sopranos or altos. It was for them that the composers extended their greatest efforts. These singers were masters of what might be called *stile fiorito,* the flowery style that dominated the eighteenth century, in which the melodic line was extravagantly ornamented with embellishments which we have come to associate with the term coloratura today. In the eighteenth century every singer of whatever range or sex was a master of such technique, so that the term coloratura as we use it today had little meaning then. Another misnomer is the term *bel canto,* beautiful singing, which we often apply today to voices untrained in the flowery style. The eighteenth century did not know the term. It was something coined in the nineteenth century to distinguish the Italian style from that being written by that upstart, Richard Wagner.

Among the most distinguished composers of Italian opera in the mid-eighteenth century were such Italianate Germans as Johann Adolph Hasse (1699-1783) and Karl Heinrich Graun (1704-1759). Native Italians included Niccolò Jommelli (1714-1774) and Tommaso Traëtta (1727-1779).

Gluck and the Reform of the Opera

Under the influence of drama as depicted on stage and television today the twentieth-century opera goer expects something far more intense dramatically than the eighteenth-century opera gives us. We lose patience with a work that only glorifies the art of the singer and singing. Yet we must not forget that this style prevailed for more than one hundred fifty years precisely because the public demanded it. However, from time to time, reforms of current operatic style were proposed. Surprisingly enough most proposed reforms have to do with the libretto —the text of the opera—rather than the music itself.

One of the most important of these so-called reform movements occurred in the 1760's. Under the influence of his librettist, Christoph Willibald Gluck (1714-1787) wrote operas which were to have some influence on the course of serious opera. Gluck began his career as a chamber musician to Prince Lobkowitz in Vienna in 1736. Here he made the acquaintance of the most famous of opera librettists, Metastasio, the imperial court poet in Vienna. In 1737 Gluck went to Italy to study under a great master of instrumental music, Giovanni Sammartini (1698-1775), from whom he acquired a sound technique of composition in the Italian style. Although Sammartini was not himself a composer of operas (he wrote only two), he showed Gluck the latent possibilities of symphonic music in opera. During his sojourn in Italy Gluck wrote several operas in the contemporary style based largely on librettos of Metastasio. After visits to London, Paris, and Copenhagen, and conducting a traveling Italian opera company in Germany, he returned to Vienna to become director of the court opera from 1754 to 1764. In 1750 he married Marianne Pergin, the daughter of a Viennese merchant. The substantial dowry which Marianne brought to the marriage seemed to encourage a kind of independence in Gluck.

It was during this period of Gluck's life that he met Raniero de' Calzabigi (1714-1795), an Italian poet-diplomat at the Viennese court, in 1761. Calzabigi led the revolt against Metastasio and the smothering conventions of the old-fashioned serious opera. He had read and was considerably influenced by an essay which had been published in 1755 entitled *Saggia sopra l'opera in musica* (Treatise on the Opera) by an Italian musician-scholar, Francesco Algarotti (1712-1764). In essence the contents of the essay proposed that there should be more accompanied recitatives, the type in which the orchestra participated, rather than just the harpsichord. He also felt that the consistent repetition of words and phrases in an aria was injurious to the dramatic effect. He proposed that all those brilliant vocal passages with their elaborate ornamentation did not always create the desired mood to be expressed. And finally he thought the spirit of the overture ought to be in keeping with the spirit of the drama. This last point needs some explanation. In most operas of the seventeenth and eighteenth centuries the overture served largely as a signal to the audience that the opera was about to commence, much as an electric bell serves that purpose in the concert hall today. The spirit and content of these overtures had little or nothing to do with the opera which succeeded it. Algarotti proposed that an atmosphere commensurate with the drama should be created. These ideas plus some features which Calzabigi had seen in French opera during a visit to Paris in 1750 had a profound effect on him.

The first joint collaboration of Gluck and Calzabigi was *Orfeo, ed Euridice*, with its story based on the well-known Greek legend which had served as the plot of the first opera ever written, in 1600, and subsequently many operas after that. They set out to create something like a French opera, on the model of Rameau, in Italian. It should be noted that although Italian opera was the universal type performed all over Europe, France with its intense chauvinism was the one country which retained certain national characteristics peculiar to its operas. These included a considerable amount of attention to ballet as a part of the action, choruses (generally absent from Italian opera), and a plot divided into five instead of three acts. There was not the marked difference in style between recitative and aria that characterized the Italian, and all the recitatives were accompanied by the orchestra. *Orfeo* utilizes innumerable choruses and ballets but retains the Italian division of three acts.   For the first time in Italian opera of the eighteenth century all the recitatives are orchestrally accompanied. The action is simplified to what might be described as a series of tableaux.

In line with what Algarotti had proposed, Gluck's vocal line is kept uncluttered of ornaments, and he did not permit his singers to improvise anything over the composed vocal melody. There are, however, certain conventions of Italian opera which he retained, namely the use of the *deus ex machina* device prevalent in Baroque drama to allow the tragedy to end happily and the part of Orpheus to be taken by a castrato. In the original Greek legend, it will be recalled, Eurydice, Orpheus' beloved, is bitten by a serpent and dies. Orpheus, by the magic of his music, gains admission to Hades, pleads for her return to earth, and is granted his request by Pluto with certain reservations: Orpheus is to return to earth, Eurydice will follow, but Orpheus is not to look back, for to gaze on his beloved during the ascent will be to lose her forever. As we know, during the upward journey, the temptation to see Eurydice is too great for Orpheus. He does look back, and she is lost to him. However, Calzabigi permits the god Amor to intervene in Orpheus' behalf, and the two lovers are enjoined amidst general rejoicing.

This experimental opera with its novel features—novel for current Italian practice—was given in the Burgtheater in Vienna on October 5, 1762, before an invited audience drawn largely from the nobility and intelligentsia of the city. The role of Orpheus was taken by a male contralto, Gaetano Guadagni. Today when the opera is presented, this role is given to a mezzo-soprano or contralto who appears disguised as a man.

As has been mentioned, there were dozens of operas written on the legend of Orpheus and Eurydice during the Baroque era, including the first opera, *L'Euridice,* by composer Jacopo Peri and poet Ottavio Rinuccini in 1600, and Monteverdi's masterpiece, *Orfeo,* of 1607. Unlike any of them Gluck commenced his work with a scene depicting Orpheus and his mourning friends at the tomb of Eurydice. He avoided all the preliminaries of the wedding festivities and the account thereafter of Eurydice's death by the messenger. The shepherds and nymphs, gathered around Orpheus, sing a choral lament that is one of the most poignant in all operatic literature. In the midst of this dirge the bereaved husband calls out, "Euridice!" Then follows a solemn dance which serves as a kind of trio to the choral sections which frame it. The group of mourners leaves, and Orpheus, left alone, pours out his grief in a simple strophic song, each of the three strophes being separated by recitatives. Then in a fit of despair Orpheus, in recitative, cries out his defiance of the gods and his determination to seek her in the nether world. At that moment Amor appears, explains to him how he may reach his beloved and the conditions by which he may return with her to earth.

The second act takes place between Hades and Elysium. Orpheus' approach throws the underworld into a kind of panic. He succeeds in winning the denizens over by his music, simple chords on his lyre, a simple song, "Deh! placatevi con me!" (Ah! do not threaten me!) His first attempts are interrupted by a shouting "No!" until he pacifies them. For the Paris version of 1774 Gluck wrote a Dance of the Furies which is one of the best-known movements in the opera as is the opening of the next scene in the Elysian Fields, the Dance of the Blessed Spirits, also written for the Paris version. Orpheus, in recitative, describes the wonder of the view before him: "How pure the sky, how clear the sun, what serene splendor!" The accompaniment to this recitative is masterfully written to create the illusion of an unearthly landscape. The chorus then sings:

> Here comes Eurydice!
> Turn, O fair one, to thy husband
> Who no more can bear thy absence
> From him: Heaven grant now his plea. . . .

In the third act catastrophe strikes. Eurydice is pictured with all the human foibles of the ideal wife. Not knowing the conditions under which she may return with Orpheus to earth, she cannot understand why he will not look at her and accuses him of no longer loving her. This scene is carried out in dialog in recitative style. In desperation Orpheus turns and gazes on her, and as he does so, her soul returns for the second time to the nether world. Orpheus then sings the most famous aria in the opera, "Che farò senza Euridici?" (What shall I do without Eurydice?), of which more will be said later. As his grief rises, Orpheus prepares to kill himself in order to join Eurydice. At that moment Amor again appears, disarms him, and announces that Eurydice once more return from the dead to rejoin her husband. The opera ends in a scene of general rejoicing. A series of dances is crowned with a festive chorus of shepherds and shepherdesses (in rondeau form) in which all sing the praise of triumphant love. October 5th, on which the opera was first presented, was the name-day of the Emperor Francis, a day on which it would have been inconceivable to produce a piece which had a tragic ending.

Orfeo was followed by another reform opera five years later. Calzabigi and Gluck again collaborated on *Alceste,* an opera based on another

Greek legend. This time it is the story of King Admetus who lies near death. An oracle decrees that his life may be spared if another will die in his stead. Alcestis, his wife, offers herself as the victim. Calzabigi again resorts to the *deus ex machina,* this time in the form of Apollo, who releases Alcestis from her vows, prolongs the life of Admetus, and allows the king and Alcestis a happy reunion. To the score of this opera is affixed a preface, supposedly written by Gluck but more likely the work of Calzabigi, which sets forth the credo of opera reform in this period.

The dedication opens with this statement: "Your Royal Highness: When I undertook to write the music for *Alceste,* I resolved to divest it entirely of all those abuses, introduced into it either by the mistaken vanity of singers or by the too great complaisance of composers, which have so long disfigured Italian opera and made of the most splendid and most beautiful of spectacles the most ridiculous and wearisome. I have striven to restrict music to its true office of serving poetry and by following the situations of the story without interrupting the action or stifling it with useless superfluity of ornaments. . . ." (The complete dedication may be found in Strunk, Oliver. *Source Readings in Music History,* N.Y.: Norton, 1950, pp. 673-675)

Here in this last sentence in part we have a misstatement. It is all very well for a composer to say that he will make music subordinate to the words, but in practice this can never be accomplished. If the music is good music, it will detract from the words regardless of the composer's noble aims. No song or opera is great because of the text. It is great because of its music. If the music is to be subordinate to the text, why then does Gluck take such care in giving us beautifully-rounded musical forms? Let us examine the most famous aria in *Orfeo.* It is sung by Orpheus at the moment that he realizes that he has lost his beloved Eurydice through his own impatience and impetuosity at seeing her again. In keeping with the classic principle of poise and nobility of expression, it is a superb example. The text follows:

Che farò senza Euridice?	What is left without Eurydice?
Dove andrò senza il mio ben?	Where to go without my love?
Euridice, o Dio, rispondi!	Eurydice, oh God, give answer!
Io son pure il tuo fedele!	I am still thy faithful mate!
Che farò, *etc.*	What is left, *etc.*
Euridice, ah, non m'avanza,	Eurydice! Ah, there appears
Più soccorso, più speranza,	No longer help nor hope
Nè dal mondo, nè dal ciel!	Either from earth or heaven!
Che farò, *etc.*	What is left, *etc.*

C

C minor

Eu-ri- di - ce! Eu -ri - di - ce! Ah! non ma van- za più soc -

cor - so, più spe- ran - za nè dal mon- do, nè dal

A

ciel! Che fa- rò sen-za Eu-ri - di - ce, do-ve an-drò sen-za il mio

ben? che fa- rò, do ve an- dro, che fa - rò sen- za il mio

ben? do -ve an- drò che fa - rò, che fa - rò sen-za il mio

ben, sen - za il mio ben, sen - za il mio ben?

Now let us look at the musical illustration. First of all Gluck states the opening two lines of text in a straightforward manner. Each line of poetry is made into a musical phrase. But then he needs to balance the two phrases (called a period) with another two phrases to satisfy a musical need. So he has to repeat the words. This first part we will label A. He then proceeds to the next two lines of the text with a new musical idea in a new key. Again, to round out the musical form, he must repeat words. Following this diversion, called B, Gluck repeats the whole of A verbatim. He then proceeds to the last three lines of the text. This time he seems to have a sufficient number of words so that he does not have to repeat any. The music, marked C, is in a minor key and quite unlike any that has been heard hitherto. Musically he feels compelled to return to his first idea (A) but with a slightly different close to give the aria a more conclusive ending (hence the symbol A'). What results is a kind of rondo form: A B A C A'. It shows that Gluck at least utilized a more flexible musical design rather than the incessant A B A. It is true that the composer wanted the music to be sung exactly as he had written it, without the roulades the trained singer would have added, especially on the return of the A sections.

The harmonic background is extremely simple in keeping with Rococo and Classic principles. However, the expressive element comes in the use of the *appoggiatura,* that device which results in a dissonance or discord on a strong beat of the measure (marked with an asterisk and labeled discord on the score) but which then resolves to a note of the harmony (consonance). This device becomes most important in instrumental music.

Omitted in the musical illustration here are the orchestral introduction and conclusion (called *ritornello*) using the material of A. However, no *ritornello* appears in the midst of the aria, hence Gluck's statement in the dedication, "I did not wish to arrest an actor in the greatest heat of dialogue in order to wait for a tiresome *ritornello,* nor to hold him up in the middle of a word on a vowel favorable to his voice, nor to make display of the agility of his fine voice in some long-drawn passage, nor to wait while the orchestra gives him time to recover his breath for a cadenza," is a truism.

"I have felt that the overture ought to apprise the spectators of the character of the action that is to be represented and to form, so to speak, its argument." If one will listen to the one-movement overture to *Alceste,* he will see how Gluck sets the atmosphere for the opera to follow and how the overture leads directly into Act I. This is not true, however, of the overture to *Orfeo.* But above all Gluck dispensed with the recitative accompanied only by the harpsichord. All the recitatives are orchestrally accompanied. The dedication states "that the concerted instruments should be introduced in proportion to the interest and intensity of the words, and not leave that sharp contrast between the aria and the recitative in the dialog, so as not to break a period unreasonable nor wantonly disturb the force and heat of the action." The dedication draws to a close with this assertion: "Furthermore, I believed that my greatest labor should be devoted to seeking a beautiful simplicity, and I have avoided making displays of difficulty at the expense of clearness; nor did I judge it desirable to discover novelties if it was not naturally suggested by the situation and the expression; and there is no rule which I have not thought it right to set aside willingly for the sake of an intended effect."

The opera destined to be the final collaboration of Gluck and Calzabigi was *Paride et Elena,* presented in Vienna on November 3, 1770. Although the story is drawn from Homer, it bears no resemblance to the Greek myth. It is a long progressive love plot, sensuous and passionate, which mounts to a joyous climax as the lovers, Paris and Helen, make off in a ship for Troy. Helen, in Calzabigi's version, is here not even the wife of Menelaus! Perhaps this was a way of circumventing the criticism of the prudish Austrian censors. The production was a failure, and although it had some twenty performances in Vienna that year, its failure no doubt led to the dissolution of one of the great partnerships in operatic history. Calzabigi returned to his native Italy shortly after. Whatever else he may have done, Calzabigi made his text simple, direct, and touching—quite different qualities from the typical Metastasian libretto.

Paris was the leading cultural center of Europe. Gluck was drawn to the possibilities there to advance his career. He had enjoyed success as a composer and producer of French comic opera at the Viennese court. François du Roullet, an attaché at the French embassy in Vienna, persuaded Gluck to go to Paris. He supplied the composer with his first libretto for a serious French opera, *Iphigénie en Aulide,* an adaptation of Racine's drama. Gluck also had a champion in Marie Antoinette, the new dauphine of France, daughter of Maria Theresa of Austria and a pupil of Gluck in singing and harpsichord playing. He left Vienna in 1773 and arrived in Paris during the midst of a controversy on the merits of French serious opera (*tragédie lyrique*) and Italian comic opera, a rather paradoxical comparison—like multiplying oranges and apples. Through the most diplomatic maneuvers and with the aid of Du Roullet and Marie Antoinette, Gluck succeeded in mounting *Iphigénie en Aulide* at the Opéra on April 19, 1774. Its success was far greater than the composer had hoped for. Almost overnight Gluck became something of an idol. *Iphigénie* combined elements of French and Italian opera and proved Rousseau wrong when the philosopher stated in his *Letter on French Music* (1753) that "there is neither measure nor melody in French music, because the language is not capable of them. . . ."

Gluck followed up his launching of *Iphigénie* with the revision for the French public of his *Orfeo*. Since the French could not tolerate the castrato, the part of Orpheus was recast for a tenor, thus necessitating some changes of key and other vocal adjustments. The composer also added further music to allow for more ballets in keeping with French taste. The text was translated from the original Italian to French. This revision has led to confusion in both modern printed editions and performances. Sometimes one hears the work sung in French with a female mezzo or contralto in the part of Orpheus or a tenor singing the lead in Italian. *Orfeo* (*Orphée et Eurydice* in French) was presented on August 2, 1774, with great success and was followed by a revision of *Alceste* in Du Roullet's French translation on April 23, 1776. Like *Iphigénie*, *Orphée* was extremely successful and heaped kudos on its composer. But Gluck's success with the French public heaped wrath on the composer by a group of literati who engaged the services of an Italian composer, Nicola Piccinni (1728-1800), to combat the Viennese upstart. This precipitated the famous quarrel of the Gluckists and Piccinnists in the Parisian press. The opera-going public was sharply divided between those who favored the pure serious opera style of the Italians and those who supported the new operatic "realism" of Gluck. Piccinni, an innocent victim of this *querelle célèbre*, represented in his operas that element which many desired: melody simply accompanied. Gluck, on the other hand, displayed more dramatic declamation and an underlying orchestral accompaniment of more significance. To keep the quarrel alive it was decided that both composers must write an opera on the same libretto and thereby determine which was the better. The libretto chosen was *Roland* by the seventeenth-century poet Quinault. Quinault had prepared the text from Ariosto's *Orlando furioso* for France's most distinguished Baroque composer, Lully. But Gluck would have no part in the scheme. He chose instead to write an opera on another libretto of Quinault, *Armide* (1686), based on Tasso's *Gerusalemme liberata*. Gluck's *Armide* was presented on September 23, 1777. It is a strange mixture of French and Italian elements. Piccinni's *Roland* was performed four months later on January 27, 1778. Both met with equal success. The famous quarrel had ended in a draw.

Gluck divided his time between Vienna and Paris, but it was in Paris that he launched his most important works. What is generally regarded as his masterpiece, *Iphigénie en Tauride,* was premiered at the Opéra on May 18, 1779. It proved to be Gluck's greatest victory in a country torn by polemics. Strangely enough it reverts back to the lyricism prevalent in operas before the composer's own reform operas, but it bears far more personal feeling and intimacy than those of his contemporaries. There are the same wonderful orchestral effects which help to point up the dramatic situations that are often found in his previous work. Gluck's last opera, *Écho et Narcisse* (September 24, 1779), bears a close resemblance in treatment to *Orfeo*. However, it does not come up to the standard of his best works and was frankly a failure with the public. Gluck had been suffering ill health. In the fall of 1779 he returned to Vienna where he was to remain until his death in 1787.

In retrospect Gluck appears to be one of the most significant composers of serious opera in the eighteenth century, one whose music has that noble simplicity for which his era strived, who synthesized national traits much as Bach did in his music. These included spectacular scenes which embraced the ballet and chorus so dear to the French, the expressive vocal line displaying the best qualities of the human voice in the tradition of the Italians, and a combining of the symphonic achievements of the German and Italian schools. Despite the fact that Gluck created in his writing a kind of international style that would, one might surmise, appeal to the opera-going public of any country, he seems to have had little influence on his contemporaries. After the French Revolution his operas were held to be a kind of model, but by then a new spirit was emanating in art—Romanticism. And in spite of all the noble gestures expressed by Richard Wagner toward Gluck, the eighteenth-century composer was being viewed through the eyes of a romanticist. Gluck after all was a product of the age of rationalism. Then too interest in serious opera in Gluck's lifetime was waning in favor of comic opera. The significance of this is best exemplified in Mozart whose final effort in the medium was a serious Italian opera, *La clemenza di Tito* (K.621; Prague, September 6, 1791), rarely staged, and whose reputation is based exclusively on his comic operas. It is unfortunate that even though Gluck has a significant place as an important composer of operas in music history, his operas seldom appear on the contemporary stage, and then only in the light of a historical revival.

Besides Gluck and Piccinni, there are a number of other outstanding composers of serious opera in this period among whom are Antonio Sacchini (1730-1786), Antonio Salieri (1750-1825), and the composer who brings classic opera to a culmination, Luigi Cherubini (1760-1842).

SUPPLEMENTARY READING

Einstein, Alfred. *Gluck.*
————. *Mozart: His Character, His Work.* pp. 383-411.
Grout. *A History of Western Music.* pp. 426-431.
————. *A Short History of Opera.* Vol. 1, pp. 181-245.
Láng. *Music in Western Civilization.* pp. 553-567.
Strunk, Oliver. *Source Readings in Music History.* The Dedication in *Alceste,* pp. 673-675.
Ulrich, Homer, and Paul A. Pisk. *A History of Music and Musical Style.* pp. 331-340; 402-403.

SUGGESTED LISTENING

Although belonging to the late Baroque, Handel's operas serve as models for the international style which prevailed in serious opera through most of the eighteenth century. Selections from these operas give only a hint of style. It is well to listen to an entire opera chosen from the following: *Alcina, Julius Caesar, Rodelinda, Serse,* and *Sosarme.*

Two operas of Gluck still remain in the standard repertory, *Orfeo* and *Alceste.* These with the aid of a libretto and the description of *Orfeo* in this book should serve as a guide.

Some of the most beautiful music Mozart wrote is contained in his serious operas. *Idomeneo* and *La clemenza di Tito,* the latter still based on a Metastasian text, are recommended for listening. It might be well to compare one of the Handel with a Mozart opera from the standpoint of recitative, types of aria, orchestration, and demands on the singer.

COMIC OPERA

Italy

Operas with comic plots came into existence as early as 1619 in Rome. Even serious operas, from 1650 on, incorporated scenes of comic relief much as such scenes occur in the tragedies of Shakespeare. Generally a pair of comic characters appeared in the cast drawn largely from the servant class—manservant, page, maidservant, nurse. From around 1685-1690 these comic episodes consistently appeared as the final scene of the first two acts and midway in the third, always having some connection, even though slight, with the plot of the serious opera. The comic scenes offered a decided contrast in subject and in musical material to the high-blown heroics and the often stylized technical virtuosity of the serious opera in which they appeared. Not until the early years of the eighteenth century did full-length comic operas again become a standard form of operatic production.

Two separate and distinct streams of development took place: the *commedia per musica* and the *intermezzo*. Naples took the lead in the early production of both types, creating almost all of the *commedie* and some seventy to seventy-five new *intermezzi* during the first half of the century. To understand the comic opera as it appears later in the century (*e.g.*, Mozart), it is necessary to investigate each type in turn.

Let us look first at the *intermezzo*. Early in the eighteenth century the comic episodes which had appeared in the seventeenth-century serious opera were removed from any connection which they might have had with the plot and instead played between the first two acts and midway in the third during a change of scenery. Precisely when this occurred is difficult to determine. The development of the *intermezzo* appears to have gone through three stages. In the first period, 1715-1725, the episodes were short—perhaps fifteen to twenty minutes duration. Seldom, if ever, was any location of scene specified in the libretto nor any stage directions nor properties indicated. The cast generally consisted of two characters: male and female. Each character generally had two arias in each part. The second period, from 1725 to 1745, shows an increased length in the *intermezzo* with the two-act form appearing more frequently. Now we have a continuous plot connecting both parts. Some indication of scene location, properties, and required costumes reveals that these items were becoming more dramatic entities. A third character (a non-singing role) was added in 1728, and there are "walk-on" parts (guards, townspeople, etc.) around 1730. Still each character was given only two arias per act or part. Certain standard plot situations occur: the "singing lesson," which enables author and composer to indulge in parody of the serious opera of the time; the woman eagerly seeking a husband, whether a servant bent on marrying the master or an older woman who realizes that the opportunities for matrimony are fast slipping away from her; the case of mistaken identity ("the mixed-up baby"). In the third period, from 1745 to 1770, the length of the *intermezzo* is further increased. The two-act division remains consistent, but with each act, around 1750, divided into scenes as in serious opera. The works were withdrawn from their function within the framework of serious opera and became independent pieces in their own right while still bearing the descriptive designation "intermezzo." There are consistent scenic location and frequently precise stage directions. The number of characters was increased (the first such added role appears in 1745), making possible lengthier and more complex ensembles at the close of each act. More arias might be given to the characters in each act than hitherto, and some use of ensemble such as a duet might appear in other places than at the close of an act. Nevertheless, the standard plot situations seem to prevail.

Of the many *intermezzi* written in the eighteenth century only one in our time has been revived with any frequency both on the stage and on recordings. This is Giovanni Battista Pergolesi's *La Serva Padrona* (The Servant as Mistress), an *intermezzo* in two acts which was performed between the acts of the composer's serious opera, *Il Prigioniero superbo* (The Proud Prisoner), in Naples on August 28, 1733. No doubt Pergolesi (1710-1736) was as surprised as anyone that this little filler was such a success, and were he alive today, he would be equally surprised that it has survived as the one example of *intermezzo* discussed in music classes in the twentieth century. Many are misled into believing that *La Serva Padrona* is an early example of an *intermezzo,* when in fact it is quite advanced and sophisticated. It has the typical plot and characters so frequently found in this period. A maid servant, Serpina, is determined to marry Uberto, the master of the house in which she works. With the help of a mute servant, Vespone, she contrives a plot to win over the old bachelor and succeeds in getting Uberto to marry her.

An element of realism with respect to the characters enters in the comic opera of the eighteenth century. Gone are the noble sentiments and mythological allusions. Gone too is the castrato, with the baritone or bass voice accepted in a leading role. This is all part and parcel of the changing social structure and philosophical outlook of the century. Who in his most imaginative moments would have thought an eighteenth-century author so bold as to have a servant duping his master? The peasant and the bourgeois, hitherto the laughing stock of the court comedy, have now become the heroes.

La Serva Padrona uses all the devices of serious opera: the *da capo* aria (ABA), the recitative with harpsichord support and even an accompanied recitative, the duet, used to end each of the two *intermezzi,* the whole sung throughout. In addition there is the patter song. Most of us are familiar with this in Gilbert and Sullivan comic operas of the nineteenth century. The rapid parlando style of the patter song so characteristic of the *intermezzo* is later absorbed in the episode sections of sonata-design movements in symphonies where rhythmic bustle replaces clearly-defined thematic ideas. Following is the first phrase of such a patter song sung by Uberto in *La Serva Padrona*:

The quick pace obviously creates a grotesque, humorous effect. This famous *intermezzo* was not only a delight to its audiences in the eighteenth century but is thoroughly enjoyable to audiences in our own time.

The other type of comic opera was the *commedia per musica*. This full length three-act comedy in music is found throughout the eighteenth century. It carried on the tradition of the comic opera begun in Rome and Florence in the seventeenth century and became a consistent type in Naples. Between 1710 and 1750 more than seventy-five such pieces were performed at the Teatro dei Fiorentini. Some of the best Neapolitan composers are represented in the composition of these works: Vinci, Leo, Logroscino, and Pergolesi, to name a few. Although they appear in the other Italian centers of opera, the model of the *commedia per musica* is generally Neapolitan.

In contrast to the *intermezzo* these works were in dialect, featured a rather low-type comedy, used folk song-like tunes, and all parodied the serious opera of the time. The three-act *commedia* continued after 1750, together with the expanding *intermezzo,* but it declined in importance in favor of the two-act *intermezzo*. The division of an opera into three acts was reserved for the serious opera. After 1750 both types of comic opera had many features in common, and it becomes increasingly difficult to separate one from the other in style.

In the course of the eighteenth century Italian comic opera underwent a radical change from farce to well-developed comedy. Many new features appeared in both the libretto and the music. The libretti leaned toward the sentimental or even pathetic while still retaining farcical elements. These operas were often termed *drama giocoso* (gay drama). Comic opera was in keeping with the philosophy expounded by Rousseau and his cry of "back to the natural." This meant for comic opera that the characters should be drawn from everyday life, and all the artificialities and superfluities prevalent in serious opera, including the castrato, were to be banished.

Carlo Goldoni (1707-1793) was one of the most popular librettists of Italian comic opera in the latter part of the century. It was he who began to divide the cast of characters into *parte serie* and *parte buffe* (serious and comic characters). Hence it becomes difficult to determine, in many respects, whether a work like Mozart's *Don Giovanni* is really tragic or comic—a tragedy with comic overtones or a comedy with serious overtones.

Mozart's Italian Operas

Wolfgang Amadeus Mozart's (1756-1791) last three Italian comic operas include *Le nozze di Figaro* (The Marriage of Figaro; K.492; Vienna, 1786), in which a barber is the hero; *Don Giovanni* (K.527; Prague, 1787), designated by Mozart as a *dramma giocoso;* and *Cosi fan tutte* (So do they all! K.588; Vienna, 1790), the story concerned with masquerade and mistaken identity so prevalent in the eighteenth century. It is with these masterpieces that the climax of the Italian comic opera is reached.

What made Mozart a cut above his contemporaries was the care he lavished on the orchestra in the accompaniment to the vocal music. Nowhere in the history of opera has there been such perfect balance between orchestral and vocal forces. This is due to the eighteenth-century development of symphonic music in Italy and the Germanic countries of which much will be said later. In Italy the vocal line in opera was exploited to the abandonment of all other factors, with the orchestra reduced to an extremely simple chordal accompaniment. At the opposite side of the spectrum, in Wagner's operas of the nineteenth century, the orchestra is the chief protagonist and the vocal parts seemingly reduced to a mere commentary.

don giovanni

When *Le nozze di Figaro* had its premiere in Vienna on May 1, 1786, it met with little success. However, when it was presented in Prague in December of that year, it met with enthusiastic response, so much so that the composer was invited to that Bohemian city by the Bondini company, which had performed *Le nozze* there, to write a new opera for the coming season. Mozart consulted with the librettist with whom he had collaborated in the production of *Le nozze*, Lorenzo da Ponte (1749-1838), the author coming up with the story of Don Juan, one whose plot was familiar to the public both on the musical and legitimate stage since the seventeenth century. The legend had been presented in burlesque as well as in serious drama from which both romantic and even religious aspects were drawn. Audiences had been intrigued with the adventures of this fascinating nobleman who worked havoc among women, invited to supper the statue of a man he had killed, and went to hell without remorse.

Da Ponte culled his material from an opera by Giuseppe Gazzaniga (1743-1818) presented in Venice in 1787 under the title *Il Convitato di pietra* (The Stone Guest). When this same opera was presented at Lucca in 1792, its title was changed to *Don Giovanni Tenorio* (Tenorio being the Don's surname). The text was by the Italian librettist Giovanni Bertati and cast in one act. Da Ponte took over the Bertati text, expanded it into two acts like the old *intermezzo,* reduced the cast of characters to eight, and in every way made it more striking and more vigorous. In Bertati's version Donna Anna withdraws after the murder of her father to a cloister and does not reappear. Da Ponte makes her one of the three feminine protagonists, actually the counter-role to Don Giovanni.

Regardless of how apt and clever Da Ponte was in creating a libretto, it was the genius of Mozart whose music brought the drama to life. It is he who guided Da Ponte and directed the play towards deeper symbolic issues. In the light of Goldoni's division of the cast into serious and comic characters, *Don Giovanni's* dramatis personae can be classified as follows:

Parti serie	*Parti buffe*
Donna Anna (Soprano)	Leporello (Bass)
Don Ottavio (Tenor)	Zerlina (Soprano)
Il Commendatore (Bass)	Masetto (Bass)
Donna Elvira (Soprano) ?	Don Giovanni (Baritone) ?

It is difficult to determine into what category such figures as Donna Elvira and Don Giovanni should be placed. Their characterization seems to defy an exact classification. In the dramatic and operatic versions prior to Mozart's, the comic traits were pretty well distributed among all the characters. But in Mozart's opera they seem to be concentrated in Leporello. Leporello is the Don's manservant, crafty, cruel, cowardly, and the possessor of dozens more such characteristics so typical of the oldest stock character in comedy. He tries to rebel and yet obediently follows his master without a will of his own in a strange mixture of protest and admiration. Italian comic opera always included servants. Zerlina and Masetto represent this tradition. However, in Mozart's opera they contribute in large measure to the human aspects of the play. Both are naïve and ingenuous. The human aspects seem centered more on the three women. Donna Elvira, rejected by Don Giovanni and treated with disdain, turns revengeful at first then heroic at the end. She is confused, insecure, and erratic in her actions. Donna Anna, on the other hand, is dignified, willful, and to her insignificant but beloved fiancé, Don Ottavio, harsh and cool. She seems to display her emotions only when defending her honor or deploring her father's death. Zerlina is the gracious, charming little peasant girl, good-natured and sincere, who is easily flattered by the attention from a *grand seigneur*. Then there is the Don himself, a suave evil-doer, the enemy of virtue and humanity, but the personage who dominates the action. He is forever present; even when not on stage he is a topic of conversation. Everybody and everything revolve around him: Donna Anna and Don Ottavio postpone their marriage; Elvira is resigned to being humiliated; for the sake of a brief and hopeless romance Zerlina almost deserts Masetto. All these people are powerless to withstand his diabolical fascination, all, that is, except one: the Commendatore whom the Don kills and who returns as a ghost. He is a superhuman force who symbolizes the power of right over wrong, the intellect over the flesh. When he stamps into the banquet hall in the last act, heralded by those marvelous harmonies which Mozart conjured up, human concerns vanish before the power of the supernatural. In his operas Mozart does not develop the characters through his music. They reveal themselves at once in an aria and remain consistent throughout the opera. The one exception in *Don Giovanni* is Donna Elvira. There are so many facets of her personality and she is such a complex figure that no one aria could do justice in revealing her character.

The overture which opens the opera is in sonata-form (see pages 57-60) as we might expect in the period and with the clarity so characteristic of Mozart. There is a slow introduction in the key of D minor, utilizing material associated with the appearance at the close of the opera of the Commendatore's statue. The mood created is one of tragedy and impending doom, a strange mood indeed for the prelude to a comic opera. However, as soon as the Main Theme of the Exposition is sounded, a festive and lively state of being is created which continues to the end of the overture. None of the themes in the main body is derived from the opera itself. The overture leads directly into the first scene. It is night, and we find Leporello pacing restlessly up and down outside the garden of the Commendatore. Mozart's music serves in many ways to divulge stage directions which in other operas would need textual explanations in the score. Take the *ritornello* which opens Leporello's aria:

This theme also serves as a kind of introduction to the short three-part aria which Leporello sings in which he denounces the state in which he finds himself as a servant—irregular meals, lack of sleep, and constant waiting around. He reflects on his master who is at that moment seducing Donna Anna in her bedroom. In the dark of the night Don Giovanni, disguised as Don Ottavio, her fiancé, reaches the summit of his desires. Donna Anna has come to the realization of the terrible truth of her betrayal. Leporello is interrupted by the sound of people approaching. Donna Anna appears in the courtyard holding firmly to Don Giovanni's arm and berating him for so deluding her. As she tries to tear the mask from his face, she calls for help. Her father, the Commendatore, appears with sword in hand. Donna Anna releases her hold on Don Giovanni and rushes back into the house. The Commendatore challenges the Don to fight. Hesitant at first because of the governor's advanced age, the Don is goaded on by the Commendatore. Leporello cowers in a corner anticipating the outcome. The music during the quarrel and the duel is intensely dramatic, again not the sort at all one would expect to find in a comic opera. The older man is mortally wounded. As he lies dying, we have an ensemble, a *terzetto,* for three bass voices, unique in the literature. This is the close of the prelude to the *dramma giocoso.*

The gloom does not prevail for long. A dialog in recitative between Don Giovanni and Leporello restores the comic mood. As they take their leave, Donna Anna returns from the house with Don Ottavio and the servants bearing torches to discover her father's body. In a dramatically accompanied recitative she swears to avenge his death and makes Don Ottavio promise to bring the unknown murderer to justice. Don Ottavio comforts Donna Anna saying, "Forget the bitter memories, for you have both a lover and father in me." With a tender, brief duet the scene comes to an end. In renouncing Don Giovanni as the murderer of her father, however, she cannot tell Don Ottavio the whole truth.

Scene 2 finds Don Giovanni and Leporello on a street. It is dawn. In the banter which follows, Leporello casually mentions bringing the catalog of the Don's conquests, which Leporello carries, up to date. Just then a woman approaches. Hiding in a doorway the men overhear her lamenting the treachery of a faithless lover. She is angry and humiliated and determined to find him. When she does find him, she will inflict terrible torture on him. The Don, with contemptuous pity, says to Leporello, "Poor girl, we must console her." Leporello cynically replies, "That's how eighteen hundred poor girls have already been consoled." As she approaches the doorway where the Don and Leporello are hiding, Don Giovanni steps out and politely addresses the woman. Immediately on seeing her he recognizes her as Donna Elvira, a former conquest, and she recognizes him as the one on whom she would wreak vengeance. The scene which follows is in the best Italian comedy tradition. The *recitativo secco* in which all three engage in rapid conversation moves at breakneck speed. The Don looks for some means of escape. He says he can explain everything and Leporello here can confirm his reasons for deserting her. Leporello produces the little black book, the catalog of conquests, and proceeds to read from it. This is one of the most famous arias in the opera and is cast in a two-part design. Cruelly, Leporello reads from the catalog a list of all the women Don Giovanni has seduced: 640 in Italy, 231 in Germany, a hundred in France . . . "But in Spain," and here Leporello pauses with pride, "in Spain no fewer than a thousand and three." In part two of the aria, the tempo changes from an *allegro* to an *andante* in which Leporello describes the Don's tastes in women. When Leporello began reading from the catalog, Don Giovanni took the opportunity to escape unnoticed. At the close of the aria, Donna Elvira, in recitative, says, "And this is the man I trusted." She swears she will be avenged. Despite her mistreatment at his hands one has the feeling that she still loves him.

Scene 3 takes us to the open country around Don Giovanni's palace. Here a group of peasants is celebrating the coming wedding of Zerlina and Masetto. It is upon this gala that Don Giovanni and Leporello make their appearance. Don Giovanni, with his eyes feasting on Zerlina, invites the peasants to his nearby estate for a tour of the grounds and rooms and to partake of refreshment. He, the Don, will personally escort Zerlina. Masetto is infuriated, and in an aria, "Ho capito" (Of course, Sir), he bitterly succumbs to the nobleman's suggestion. Don Giovanni succeeds in getting Zerlina alone in the only scene of the opera in which his technique as a lover is revealed. He flatters her with a promise of marriage, and in the duet, "Là ci darem la mano" (There you will give me your hand and consent), we have some of the most seductive music Mozart ever wrote. Just as the Don seems to have made his conquest and is leading her toward the little summer house, Donna Elvira suddenly makes her appearance, denounces Don Giovanni, and congratulates herself for having arrived at an opportune time to rescue an innocent girl. After a brief aria in Handelian style, "Ah! fuggi il traditor!" (The traitor means deceit), Donna Elvira sweeps out taking Zerlina away with her under her protection.

As the Don stands alone somewhat bewildered, wondering what went wrong, Donna Anna, dressed in mourning, and Don Ottavio approach him. Donna Anna has come to enlist the services of Don Giovanni in seeking out the murderer of her father. She does not recognize the Don as her seducer. Don Giovanni for a moment is startled with the situation but quickly regains his composure. Suddenly Donna Elvira enters. She starts the quartet ensemble by warning Donna Anna against this man. Don Giovanni counters with the assertion that the woman is mad, and indeed her agitation is such that it looks at first as if the Don is right. As the quartet proceeds, Donna Anna and Don Ottavio begin to have their suspicions about the Don. This ensemble is a great example of Mozart's unique understanding of the power of music over drama: the power to present several points of view by the characters simultaneously. Only in opera could such a procedure be made possible.

In a recitative Don Giovanni adopts the caressing tone of the experienced lover when he says, "Forgive me, dear lady, if I take my leave now. . . ." It is at this moment that Donna Anna recognizes the Don as her assailant and her father's murderer. Anna relates to Ottavio in recitative the events of the night before but claims she escaped from the Don before her honor was violated. From accounts we have, the eighteenth-century audiences found this a particularly hilarious scene, especially when Don Ottavio says, "Respiro" (I breathe again). In the marvelous aria which follows she persuades Don Ottavio to avenge her father's death. Donna Anna leaves the stage, and Ottavio sings an aria which was added to the original score for the Vienna performance, "Dalla sua pace la mia depende" (On her peace of mind mine too depends). It expresses as does a later aria his dog-like devotion. At his exit Leporello appears on the scene again grumbling and threatening to quit his master's employ. Soon the Don enters in a gay mood. They take a moment to compare notes on their respective adventures. The Don plans to invite all the peasants to a party within the next few hours. With an atmosphere filled with tension and excitement he sings the famous "Champagne Aria." The orchestration is dazzling. Mozart uses all the woodwinds *in toto* for the first time since the overture. Don Giovanni is sure he can add several names to his catalog among the peasantry before morning.

The final scene in this act is set in the garden of Don Giovanni's palace. A crowd of peasants is wandering about the grounds. Zerlina and Masetto are arguing. Masetto accuses Zerlina of being unfaithful. Zerlina counters with an aria of marvelous simplicity, "Batti, batti, o bel Masetto" (Beat me, beat me, dear Masetto). The tempo and meter change; Zerlina cries, "Peace," and promises that their days and nights will be spent in happiness and contentment. Masetto seems pacified. But when Zerlina hears Don Giovanni's voice, she becomes nervous and seeks some place to hide. She wants to avoid the embarrassment of meeting the Don in the presence of her betrothed.

The Finale of the first act now begins. The ensemble-finale was treated with special care by all composers of comic opera but none more meticulously than Mozart who considered key relationship, thematic material, and organization as he would in composing a symphony. Not only is the ensemble a means of obtaining vocal sonority, but Mozart succeeds in maintaining the qualities of each of the characters so that the actor's identity in the group is never lost. The organization of the Finale with its key scheme can be charted out something like this:

Section 1	Section 2	Section 3	Section 4
Allegro assai	Andante	Allegretto	Menuetto
C major; C meter	F major; 3-4	F major to	F major; 3-4
		D minor; 2-4	
			Note relationship

Section 5	Section 6	Section 7	Section 8
Adagio	Allegro	Maestoso	Menuetto
B-flat major;	E-flat major; 6-8	C major; 2-4	G major; 3-4
C meter			

Section 9 (a compound section)

Allegro assai	Andante maestoso	Allegro
E-flat major and	C major	A major
modulatory		
C meter throughout		

In Section 1 Masetto tells Zerlina that he will conceal himself to see what happens when Don Giovanni meets her. The Don with an entourage of servants approaches the peasants who have been relaxing on the lawn and orders the servants to escort the peasants indoors for a party. When they have left, Zerlina and the Don remain alone. Zerlina, in Section 2, is frightened and tries to hide among the trees, but Don Giovanni sees her and catches her by the hand. Seductively he tries to lead her to the arbor. As they reach the spot, Masetto shows himself, much to the Don's surprise and consternation. He quickly recovers his poise and tells Masetto how concerned Zerlina has been with his absence. The sound of music (Section 3) coming from Don Giovanni's palace prompts him to suggest that Masetto and Zerlina join the others at the party, an invitation eagerly accepted by them, and all depart. The music now changes to minor as three masked figures appear on the grounds. They are Donna Elvira, Donna Anna, and Don Ottavio. They are masked for the purpose of disguise, not to attend a masked ball as so many believe. An agitated orchestral motive accompanies the trio as they speak of seeking their revenge that night, though Donna Anna has some perturbation and fears for her fiancé.

Section 4 brings us the music of the most famous minuet ever written. With the minuet sounding in the background, Leporello, looking out the window of the palace and observing the three masked figures, draws the Don's attention to them. Don Giovanni orders Leporello to invite them in. After the invitation Leporello closes the window, thus shutting out the sound of the minuet.

Section 5 introduces solemn music. Donna Anna, Donna Elvira, and Don Ottavio remove their masks and wend their way toward the palace. They reflect on the situation in which they find themselves. Donna Anna is not quite so frightened now as Don Ottavio tries to bolster her courage. Donna Elvira prays that heaven will avenge the betrayer of her love. Mozart accompanies this trio with wind instruments only (flutes, oboes, clarinets, bassoons, horns).

Section 5 has ushered us into a lavish hall of the palace. Lively music (Section 6) from three stage orchestras now serves as a background for the party. The dance has concluded, and Don Giovanni assists the peasant girls to their seats. He flirts openly with Zerlina much to the displeasure of Masetto. When the three guests arrive, they have replaced their masks and are cordially welcomed by Leporello and the Don. The dance resumes (Sections 7 and 8). Actually there are three dances going on apparently in three different rooms: a minuet for the aristocracy, a waltz, and, for the lower classes, a country dance. Don Giovanni tries to abduct Zerlina from the ballroom. Suddenly a cry escapes from Zerlina. The orchestra in the pit resumes its role with agitated dramatic music (Section 8). Everyone's attention is drawn toward Zerlina and the Don. Don Giovanni's first reaction is to draw his sword and to make Leporello the scapegoat as if it were he, Leporello, who had abducted Zerlina (Section 9). However this feint does not fool the others. Donna Anna, Donna Elvira, and Don Ottavio remove their masks and are at once recognized by Don Giovanni who is denounced as a deceiver. Don Ottavio levels a pistol at the culprit. Exactly what happens at this moment neither Da Ponte nor Mozart makes clear in the score. Don Giovanni declares amidst the threats that he fears nothing and nobody. As the curtain falls, Don Giovanni is seen escaping with Leporello through the crowd unscathed.

When the curtain opens on Act II, Don Giovanni and Leporello are seen on a street, opposite of which stands Donna Elvira's house with a balcony. The liveliness of the music reveals at once that the Don is his old self and that what has transpired before has had no effect on him. Leporello again threatens to leave the Don's service, but Don Giovanni proffers money to soothe his servant's anguish. The Don explains his next plan. He, the Don, wishes to seduce Donna Elvira's maid. Since he surmises that he can more easily do this by being garbed as a servant, he persuades Leporello to exchange cape and hat with him. All of the above has taken place in a recitative dialog. Then Donna Elvira makes her appearance on the balcony. It is growing dark. In one of the most beautiful trios of the opera Donna Elvira first reflects on her bewildered feelings, both loving and hating the Don. Don Giovanni answers her in the same musical style. He flatters her with endearments, and she leaves her balcony to join the man she thinks is her lover. Of course one must realize that the Don's motive is to get to the maid. When Donna Elvira arrives on the street, Leporello, disguised as the Don, runs toward her, kisses her, imitates his master's voice, and removes her from the scene. Don Giovanni then sings his serenade, "Come to the window," in the tradition of an Italian song of his time with mandolin accompaniment. On completion of the serenade Don Giovanni is suddenly interrupted by the arrival of Masetto leading a band of armed peasants determined to kill the Don. Since Don Giovanni is disguised as a servant and hence unrecognizable as the lord of the manor, he offers to aid them in their search—all in the musical style associated with Leporello. Directing the peasants to split up he takes Masetto aside to learn of his intentions. With the flat of his sword Don Giovanni begins to beat Masetto unmercifully. Now Zerlina appears with a lantern to discover her fiancé alone and groaning with pain. A tender but comic scene ensues in which Masetto exaggerates his injuries, and Zerlina consoles him. In a very touching aria, "Vedrai, carino" (You will see, beloved, if you are good, what a fine remedy I have), she confirms her love for Masetto.

Scene 2 takes place in the courtyard of Donna Anna's palace. Leporello hurriedly leads Donna Elvira to the courtyard away from the mob of peasants outside. She still thinks she is with Don Giovanni and wonders why he seems so frightened. Leporello's aim is to escape in the darkness, but he cannot find an exit. Elvira, alarmed at discovering herself alone, begins the famous sextet, "Alone in this darkness I feel my heart beating. . . ." This sextet, like Mozart's finales, is a panorama of action on stage without interrupting the smooth musical flow which the composer has in mind. There are changes of key, tempo, and meter to suit the activity, but the musical sequence is always logical. Donna Elvira's opening phrase is interrupted by Leporello's frustrated comic-patter while seeking an exit. A sudden modulation of key heralds the arrival of Donna Anna and Don Ottavio with a retinue of servants carrying torches. Don Ottavio consoles Donna Anna in her grief, for she is still mourning the death of her father. As Donna Elvira rushes about the darkness seeking whom she believes to be Don Giovanni, Leporello finally sees a doorway at the same time that Elvira does, and both head toward it. When they reach it, the door is opened by Zerlina and Masetto who prevent Leporello from leaving, crying, "Stop, villain!" Donna Anna and Don Ottavio converge on the group and, believing Leporello to be the Don, demand his death. But Donna Elvira pleads for mercy for the man she now calls her husband. Her entreaties go unheeded. Don Ottavio draws his sword to kill the culprit. Leporello falls to his knees in supplication. And while being a serio-comic scene, Mozart wrote the music in G minor thus creating genuine pathos. Of course the masquerade is exposed to the perplexity of the ensemble standing there. The tempo changes to *molto allegro* and the assembled company reflects on the extraordinary day it has experienced. (It must be realized that the entire action of the opera takes place in a twenty-four-hour period.)

Donna Anna retires; the rest turn on poor Leporello and, in recitative, berate him. Don Ottavio declares that he will seek the proper authorities who will bring the murderer of the Commendatore to justice. After the recitative he sings one of the most exquisite arias in operatic literature, "Il mio tesoro" (Meanwhile, go and console my dear one). Zerlina is not quick to forgive, and brandishing a knife she pulls Leporello about by the hair. With the help of a peasant she ties him to a chair. When all have left, Leporello manages to slip from his bonds and escape. Zerlina returns with Donna Elvira to show her how Leporello has been punished. Much to her chagrin she finds he has eluded her. Left alone, Donna Elvira sings a recitative and aria of self-pity with some noteworthy poignant passages by Mozart. Were it not for Mlle. Cavalieri who sang in the first Viennese performance of the opera and who insisted that Mozart write for her a *scena* commensurate with her talent and artistic importance, we would never have had this aria, "Mi tradi quell' alma ingrata" (I was betrayed by that ungrateful soul), which concludes the scene.

With Scene 3 the action recommences. Don Giovanni, still disguised as Leporello, leaps over the wall of an enclosed churchyard where several statues stand including one in the image of the late Commendatore. Soon Leporello turns up in the cemetery seeking refuge from his recent escape in the courtyard. He is distraught with the situation in which he finds himself and surprised to see the Don. As Leporello and the Don exchange clothes and discuss their recent adventures with some amusement, the sinister voice of the Commendatore's statue proclaims, "You will not laugh after dawn!" For the first time someone of authority takes Don Giovanni to task for his misdeeds. The statue's pronouncement is accompanied dramatically in part by three trombones, this color long associated in the mind of the eighteenth-century audience with the supernatural and the solemnly religious. Don Giovanni and Leporello believe the voice to be that of a prankster concealed in the foliage. After prodding among the headstones with his sword, the Don comes upon the statue of the Commendatore. Once more the statue speaks, warning Don Giovanni to let the dead lie in peace. The Don stoops to read aloud the inscription carved below the statue: "Vengeance here awaits the villain who took my life." With this Leporello becomes terrified. "O vecchio buffonissimo!"—"the old fool," says Don Giovanni, and commands Leporello to invite the statue to supper at his home. With reluctance but with exaggerated politeness Leporello relays his master's request. This action is fulfilled in a duet which Mozart writes for Leporello and Don Giovanni. The statue, with a simple "yes," accepts the Don's invitation. With that Leporello and Don Giovanni leap over the wall and are gone.

The curtain rises on Scene 4 to reveal a gloomy room in what may be assumed to be Donna Anna's palace. There, in recitative, Don Ottavio is consoling the mourning Donna Anna. In expressing his love for her he seems a slightly less insipid figure than before. But Anna rebukes him. How can he press his suit at a time like this? Don Ottavio, his patience growing short, accuses her of being cruel. After a short accompanied recitative, Donna Anna sings an aria, "Non mi dir" (Do not tell me, beloved, that I am cruel to thee), cast in a simple A B A design. It is a rather bland but elegant aria and suggests the character of Donna Anna under normal circumstances rather than the excited condition under which we have viewed her from the start. A coda moving at a swifter tempo and in coloratura style brings the aria to a close. It succeeds in setting off the egocentric character of this prima donna.

And now in Scene 5 we come to another great ensemble-finale by Mozart. It is set in the brightly-lighted banquet hall of Don Giovanni's palace. A flourish of trumpets and drums sets the mood. Believing the whole affair of a statue's coming to dinner to be improbable, the Don looks greedily at the sumptuous meal spread out on the table. He directs the musicians of his band to commence playing. The first selection is an excerpt from Martin y Soler's opera, *Una cosa rara*, a work which had been extremely successful in its recent Viennese premiere. The band's next piece is the Scoffing Song from Sarti's *I due litiganti,* an opera heard in Prague in 1783. During the interval of stage music Don Giovanni samples morsels of food from the table. Finally the band plays "Non più andrai" from Mozart's own *Figaro* to which the Don remarks that it is a tune much to his liking and often heard. This bit of stage gimmickry must have delighted the audience in Prague. Upon this scene Donna Elvira suddenly rushes, in a state which Da Ponte describes as "disperata." She announces that she is willing to forgive him if he will but change his way of life. To the Don's astonishment she falls to her knees, and Don Giovanni likewise falls to his knees and soothes her with exaggerated courtesy. He sings irreverently his praises of women and wine as the basis and glory of humanity. Struck by his remarks, she rises to leave. On opening the door she emits a piercing scream, staggers back into the room, and makes her escape from another exit. Don Giovanni, puzzled by this further interruption, directs Leporello to go to the door to see what it is all about. On opening the door Leporello too lets out a yell, locks the door, and backs away into the room speechless.

In a new tempo and meter (Section 3 of the Finale) Leporello breathlessly relates that the "stone man, the white man" stands outside, and tries to describe him to the Don. Don Giovanni doesn't understand what Leporello is saying. Then a heavy knock is heard on the door. Instead of obeying his master's order to open the door, Leporello hides under the banquet table, necessitating Don Giovanni to go to the door himself. On opening it he steps back, and the statue of the Commendatore, now mobile, enters the room to a modified version of the chords first heard in the overture. Mozart in this scene maintains a tension arising from these harmonies and a musical development far beyond what is only hinted at in the overture. The dynamics of sudden alternations of *forte* and *piano* are particularly effective. "You invited me to supper," the statue begins. "Here I am." The Don, poised as ever, admits he did not expect his guest and directs the cowering Leporello to set another place at once. The statue remarks that mortal food is no longer to his taste. Don Giovanni, displaying impatience, asks, "What do you want?" The marvelous orchestral color Mozart conjures up during this scene is worthy of the listener's attention. The statue invites the Don to depart with him. Leporello begs his master not to go, but in a final heroic phrase unlike anything we have heard from him yet Don Giovanni declares that he fears nothing and that he will go with the statue. The statue grasps Don Giovanni's hand. The Don winces with the coldness of the statue's hand. "Repent and mend your ways!" thunders the statue as the tempo of the music accelerates. The statue repeats his request, and Don Giovanni continues to reply, "No!" Da Ponte's stage directions read, "Disappears. Fire from different directions, earthquake." As the flames engulf the Don, the earth opens up, a chorus of demons is heard, Don Giovanni is drawn into the gap resulting from the earthquake, and utters a final scream.

The next section of the Finale brings Donna Anna, Donna Elvira, Zerlina, Masetto, Don Ottavio, and officers of the law into the palace seeking the Don. Leporello crawls from beneath the table to inform them that his master has gone far away—a long way away.

A *larghetto* movement begins as a duet between Donna Anna and Don Ottavio in which Ottavio suggests that since their troubles are all solved, Donna Anna is free to marry him. But Donna Anna says she will consider the matter. Donna Elvira announces that she will retire to a convent. Zerlina and Masetto plan to resume their wedding dinner, and Leporello declares he will go to the village tavern to seek another but kindlier master.

In lively tempo the last section of the ensemble draws all the characters in a typical moralizing finale in which is reflected the dictum that the mortal punishment of the wicked fits their crime. The contrapuntal style which Mozart used for the sextet makes this ensemble sound more profound than the text would imply.

Mozart's contemporaries in the area of Italian comic opera include Pasquale Anfossi (1727-1797), Niccola Piccinni, Giovanni Paisiello (1740-1816) who wrote a *Barbieri di Siviglia* (1782) long before Rossini, and Domenico Cimarosa (1749-1801). Most of their works were premiered either in Italy or Vienna.

English Ballad Opera

When Handel arrived in England in 1710, Italian serious opera already had a strong foothold. After the death of Henry Purcell in 1695, England had no outstanding creative talent to combat the invasion of Italian composers and singers. The country simply succumbed to foreign influences, and due largely to Handel's, Bononcini's, and Porpora's efforts, Italian serious opera took the English public by storm. Attendance at operatic performances became the most fashionable pastime of an affluent society. Such enthusiasm for a foreign art was destined in time to provoke a reaction. This reaction took the form of a type of comic opera which in part ridiculed Italian opera. It was called *ballad opera*

Hogarth, England, (1697-1764): **Laughing Audience** (Etching), Museum of Fine Arts, Boston.

because it utilized ballad tunes well known to the English populace from collections of folk and popular songs of the British Isles. To these tunes were set new words in keeping with the story depicted.

The most famous of these ballad operas was the first ever staged, *The Beggar's Opera*. It was produced at Lincoln's Inn Fields Theatre on January 29, 1728, ran for sixty-two nights the first season, and had the most performances of any production in the eighteenth century. The libretto was written by John Gay (1685-1732), a good-natured wit who numbered among his friends the literary giants of England and nearly all the titled ladies of the kingdom. In keeping with some of the literature of the period, its language is low and racy. Gay collaborated with Johann Christoph Pepusch (1667-1752), a German composer who had settled in London around 1700. Since the tunes were already chosen, many no doubt by Gay and his friends, Pepusch's task was largely that of an arranger, preparing suitable orchestral accompaniments to the airs and composing an overture. The sixty-nine ballads and dance tunes, some dating from Elizabethan times, are full of charm and appear perfectly natural in the course of the work. *The Beggar's Opera* must be described as a play with music rather than an opera. The dialog is spoken in contradistinction to the Italian comic opera, which is sung throughout. The plot tells of Macheath, a highwayman, who marries Polly Peacham, daughter of the fence with whom the thieves do business, much to her parent's chagrin. Polly's mother succeeds in a scheme to have Macheath arrested. He is brought to Newgate prison where Lucy, daughter of the jailer, helps him to escape in the hope that Macheath will marry her. To free himself from his dilemma of being married to one girl though longing to marry another, he surrenders himself to the police and resigns himself to being hanged. But the Beggar and the Player who appeared briefly in the Prolog serve as the *deus ex machina* and intervene in his behalf. Macheath and Polly are reunited. So much besides opera is satirized—politics, marriage, to name two subjects— that Sir Robert Walpole, Britain's prime minister, forbade Gay's sequel entitled *Polly* to be performed. But dozens of other operas in their vein, utilizing ballad tunes, were written. The sources of good ballads were soon exhausted, and composers wrote songs of their own. However none had that particular charm that made the public take Gay's work to its heart, and although *The Beggar's Opera* did much to upset Italian opera production in London for awhile, its creation was short-lived and seemed to lead up a blind alley. However, it reflected that naturalism so ardently desired in the eighteenth century.

French Opéra-Comique

French comic opera was already in existence in the 1660's when Jean-Baptiste Lully (1632-1687) collaborated with Molière to create the *comédie-ballet* which alternated songs and dances with spoken dialog. When Lully began to consider writing serious opera, the *tragédie lyrique*, in the 1670's, he gained, through royal dispensation, a virtual monopoly over opera productions in France. The letters patent of Louis XIV directed that no theater in Paris could employ more than two singers and six orchestral players. To circumvent this decree a company such as the Italian Theater in residence in Paris, which had depended so much on its musical features, began using simple songs which the actors could easily encompass. These songs were often well-known popular songs to which new words were written and were called *vaudevilles*. The *vaudeville* then was not unlike the English ballad used in the ballad opera. When the Italian Theater was disbanded in 1697, its repertoire, now performed in French, was taken over by various small companies who performed largely at fairs just outside Paris.

It was out of one of these companies that the Théâtre de l'Opéra-comique, in 1715, was established. The Théâtre presented comedies in which the *vaudeville* served as the chief diversion. The Opéra, the official company presenting serious opera, forbade another company's presenting works which were sung throughout. So, like the ballad opera, we have in *opéra-comique*, the name applied to this type of entertainment, spoken dialog interspersed with simple tunes.

From time to time at the Paris Opéra there were performed Italian comic operas including *La Serva Padrona*, once in 1746 and again in 1752. The success of Italian comic opera led to a reaction in France called "Guerre des Buffonistes et Anti-Buffonistes." It was indeed a "war of buffoons," for the letters, articles, and essays which it provoked argued the merits of French serious opera *vs.* Italian comic opera—two disparate types. The former had its support among the aristocracy, the latter among the intelligentsia. It is possible that the reason why of all Italian *intermezzi La Serva Padrona* is as well known today is because of its association with those focal works performed at this time.

The upshot of performances of Italian comic opera was an interest and improvement in French efforts in comic opera. More original music, though still in the style of the *vaudeville*, was composed. The most famous example emanating from this period is Jean-Jacques Rousseau's *Le Devin du Village*, performed at Fontainebleau on October 8, 1752. It is strange, however, that this well-known work is rather atypical of

the many written in the eighteenth century. Rousseau had such a high
regard for Italian opera and such a low opinion of French opera in
general that in composing *Le Devin* he had it sung throughout, utilizing
recitatives and even using the Italian type overture. Why this work was
so popular is one of the great mysteries of music history. It had some
four hundred performances between 1752 and 1829. The plot is quite
inane. A young girl, Colette, fears that her lover, Colin, is unfaithful.
She seeks advice from the village fortuneteller who advises her to feign
indifference toward Colin. She does and wins back her lover. There
are choruses and dances typical of French opera. However, the melodies
are charming, bearing as they do a close resemblance to the *vaudeville*,
and the harmony is so simple as to be naïve.

Rousseau's success, along with the diatribes found in the pamphlets
produced during the War of the Buffoons, and a new upsurge of interest
in the English novel helped to create a distinct kind of French opera,
the *opéra-comique* which, like the Italian *dramma giocoso*, became sentimental in its plot. The quality of the music, although retaining much
of the flavor of the *vaudeville*, was greatly improved. But composers
retained the spoken dialog. Among the best-known of the *opéras-
comiques* are Duni's *Ninette a la cour* (Ninette at Court, 1755), Dani-
can's *Tom Jones* (1765), and Monsigny's *Le Déserteur* (1769). André
Ernest Modeste Grétry (1741-1813) in the latter part of the eighteenth
century created two distinct types of *opéra-comique* with respect to plot:
the fairy-tale opera (*Zémire et Azor*, 1771) and the "rescue opera"
(*Richard Coeur de Lion*, 1784), which became so popular directly after
the French Revolution.

Like the ballad opera, the *opéra-comique* seemed also to lead up a
blind alley. Opera in France at the start of the nineteenth century took
a different direction, while *opéra-comique* eventually turned toward the
operetta, best exemplified in the works of Jacques Offenbach (1819-1880).

German Singspiel

The only center of German native opera at the beginning of the
eighteenth century was Hamburg. Like England, Germany had succumbed to an Italian invasion. Almost all the larger cities and courts
performed Italian opera with Italian singers. Then with the death in
1739 of Reinhard Keiser, the director of the Hamburg Opera and its
leading composer, the collapse of native efforts was all but complete.

Around the middle of the century a new type of opera, comic in
spirit, was to make its appearance. It all got started when bands of
itinerant players traveling about the countryside discovered that if they
inserted a few songs in the course of their plays, larger audiences were

attracted. The songs had to be extremely simple for the actors to execute them.

The first significant effort to write a play with a great many songs, after the manner of the English ballad opera and French *opéra-comique,* was a work called *Der Teufel ist Los; oder, Die verwandelten Weiben* (The Devil to Pay; or, the Wives Metamorphos'd). This was a translation of a ballad opera by a popular author, Charles Coffey. The translation was made by Von Borcke, the Prussian ambassador to London, and performed in Berlin in 1743. No doubt the original ballad tunes were used on this occasion. Later another version of this opera was presented in Leipzig in 1752 with new musical settings by Standfuss. Christian Weisse, who had prepared the new version and was a well-known poet and author of children's stories, visited Paris in 1759. There he saw a number of *opéras-comiques* and with the help of Johann Adam Hiller, the cantor and Musikdirector of the Thomas-Schule in Leipzig, translated them into German and arranged many of these works as *Singspiele,* the term used to describe German comic opera. It was Hiller's idea to let the performers depicting nobility in the drama to sing elaborate arias, and those depicting characters of low social caste to sing very simple songs. This idea is important in the light of what Mozart does later. The collaboration of Hiller and Weisse in the production of some of the most successful *Singspiele* in the eighteenth century made Dresden a leading center. The simple, folk song-like tunes which Hiller wrote were sung not only all over Germany but in foreign countries as well. Weisse's librettos, drawn largely from the repertoire of French *opéras-comiques,* depicted characters from every-day life and exalted the triumph of good over evil. They glorified the peasant at a time when such glorification appealed to the people in the pre-Revolutionary period.

The popularity of the *Singspiel* spread to Berlin and then to Vienna. In 1778 Emperor Joseph II of Austria ordered the establishment of a national *Singspiel* theater in Vienna. Although a number of popular works by such composers as Karl Ditters von Dittersdorf (1739-1799) and Johann Schenk (1753-1836) were frequently presented there, the artistic peak was reached in the *Singspiele* of Mozart, especially with the first of his works to be given in the *Singspiel* theater, *Die Entführung aus dem Serail* (The Abduction from the Harem, K.384, 1782). His crowning achievement came with *Die Zauberflöte* (The Magic Flute, K.620, 1791). It uses spoken dialog in German instead of the sung recitatives prevalent in his Italian comic operas. It differentiates the social status of the characters by contrasting musical styles. Hence to a figure like Papageno, the bird catcher, who wants no more out of life than sufficient food, the comforts of a home, and a wife for companionship,

Mozart assigns a folk-like aria. As in all Mozart's operas, the initial aria
by a character generally reveals his personality at once. Here is the
opening of Papageno's aria:

Der	Vo - gel - fän - ger	bin ich ja, stets	lus - tig hei - sa hop-sa-sa!
I	am a man of	widespread fame, And	Pa - pa- ge - no is my name.

For characters representing royalty, Mozart gives them elaborate Italianate arias. The so-called Queen of the Night aria ("Der hölle Rache")
is the equal in its technical demands on the singer of any to be found
in serious opera. Like the Italian comic opera, the ensemble again is an
important aspect of the *Singspiel*.

Despite certain differences between comic operas in the various countries they all tend to draw characters from real life and often from a
lower social class, as servants. Where the plot uses characters drawn
from the nobility, they are depicted with all their human foibles and
are frequently duped by their servants. One senses in opera then another
aspect of the rising social revolution which is about to erupt. The
castrato has no place in the scheme of an opera bordering on realism.
All except the Italians use spoken dialog and all use the country's own
language. The lively musical style which accompanies these operas is
contagious and will be felt time and again in symphonic literature, especially in the symphonies of Haydn, himself a composer and producer
of comic operas.

SUPPLEMENTARY READING

Einstein. *Mozart: His Character, His Work*. pp. 412-468.
Grout. *A Short History of Opera*. Vol. 1, pp. 246-296.
Landon, H. C. Robbins, and Donald Mitchell, eds. *The Mozart Companion*.
    pp. 283-321.
Láng. *Music in Western Civilization*. pp. 547-553; 579-585.
Ulrich & Pisk. *A History of Music and Musical Style*. pp. 242-243; 340-359.

SUGGESTED LISTENING

Pergolesi. *La Serva Padrona*
Mozart. *Don Giovanni*
        La nozze di Figaro
        Die Zauberflöte
Pepusch & Gay. *The Beggar's Opera*
Rousseau. *Le Devin du Village*

As suggested in the section on serious opera, it is best to listen to these
works in their entirety rather than in excerpts.

instrumental music

INTRODUCTION: THE SONATA CONCEPT

The real dualism of the eighteenth century, and it occurs at its height in the middle of the century, is the conflict between the homophonic style (*style galant*) and counterpoint ("learned style"). Composers and aestheticians in accepting the homophonic as the prevailing and dominant style relegated the art of counterpoint to the role of a pedagogical tool or a style that seemed appropriate only to church music.

The *style galant* was characterized by (1) the clear articulation of the theme; (2) ornamentation; (3) *tempo rubato;* and (4) homophonic texture. Melody for its own sake was exploited, and the composer took pride in devising ways in which melody could be clearly set off. Ornamentation was profuse, and the composer provided his melody with dazzling runs, broken chords, and intricate figural work, all within the framework of a simple harmony. In *tempo rubato* (literally, stealing the time) the melodic line exhibits a certain flexibility in rhythm, slowing up slightly in some places and then hurrying to catch up with an accompaniment that remains steady and strict in its tempo and rhythm throughout. Singers of today's popular songs are practitioners of this. It is an expressive device in music, and this vacillation in tempo in the melody was especially desirable in mid-eighteenth-century performances by vocalists and solo instrumentalists. Harmony was kept simple so as not to intrude or detract from the theme. The most important development, however, was the gradual elimination of the whole process of thorough-bass, that Baroque device with which a bass line was provided with numbers to indicate to the performer exactly what harmony should be played at the keyboard. As we approach the middle of the eighteenth century, composers seem to resent this improvisational technique and prefer to write out the keyboard part, demanding that the performer observe closely the exact notation indicated by the composer. Then too when composers were seeking a true chamber music style—a style in which each instrument carried its own part in the ensemble—the idea of duplicating or reinforcing a part such as the bass was anathema to the composer's conception of what chamber style should be. And when the composer began to write out the inner parts of a piece and to simplify the harmony and the bass line, it spelled the doom of the old thorough-bass (or figured bass or *continuo*) technique, and a whole new concept of musical texture was born. Even in the melody composers indicated precisely how the line should be ornamented. We have seen how Gluck no longer allowed his singers to improvise ornaments in the vocal part. Composers of instrumental music became just as strict.

Where voluminous sound had been a typical trait of the Baroque, now the trend was toward a thinner, clearer instrumentation. The *style galant* era had a penchant for solo instrumentation. Even where an orchestra was required in symphonic works, a strict proportional balance in the instrumentation was observed and the number of players limited.

With the emphasis on melody and a subordinate accompaniment the formal aspects of music were duly considered. Composers of the *style galant* and Classic period used a certain guide line in compositional procedure. Taking their cue from dance forms which existed in the seventeenth century, they would write a movement of a sonata, for example, in a two-part plan, which we can symbolize as A A'. Part I (A) would initiate the basic thematic ideas. Starting in the tonic key (the home key, designated by a key signature at the head of the score) it would modulate, or change key. If the piece were in a major key, the modulation would proceed on a key five steps above the home key, called the dominant. Hence if the composer began in the key of C, which has no sharps or flats in the signature (all white notes on the piano), he would begin to change key to G, which has one sharp (counting C as 1, D as 2, E as 3, F as 4, G as 5, we thereby reach the dominant). It is on this new key that Part I (A) would end. Hence a tension is created demanding a return to the tonic. This is accomplished in Part II (A'). Using the same thematic material in much the same order as Part I, the composer would commence the new part in the dominant key (G), and by a circuitous route during which he might touch on other keys, including the minor mode, he would return to the tonic key to the satisfaction of the listener. If Part I commenced in a minor key, say A minor (no sharps or flats in the signature), he would usually modulate to the relative major (C major, no sharps or flats). Part II would then commence in C major, modulate, and return to A minor. Charted out, it looks something like this:

A	A'
PART I Tonic ⟶ Dominant	PART II Dominant ⟶ Mod. ⟶ Tonic

The composer often seemed more concerned with key relationship than he was with the thematic material itself. In time this two-part design was expanded. The modulatory portion of Part II became a separate section and the whole of A then repeated, but all in the tonic key, like this:

A	A'	A''
EXPOSITION Tonic ⟶ Dominant	DEVELOPMENT Modulatory	RECAPITULATION Tonic

Thus A exhibits duality of key, A' might exhibit multiplicity of key, and A'' unity of key. When this occurs, we have what is known as sonata-form, one of the most successful designs planned in the history of music and one which was exploited for 200 years. And although the eighteenth century did not know the term "sonata-form," the nineteenth century applied this label and went on to designate A as an Exposition (statement of thematic materials), A' as Development, and A'' as Recapitulation.

Although composers in the early stages of sonata-form were concerned primarily with the matter of key relationship, there had to be some order about the presentation of thematic material. The opening motive or theme, which we can call a Main Theme, often outlined the tonic triad for the purpose of orienting the listener to the key, as:

C. P. E. Bach: Symphony in D major, 1st movement

Haydn: Quartet in B-flat major,
Opus 1, No. 1 (HoV III:1)

When the second tonal level is reached, the composer may choose to use the same theme, now transposed to a related key, or a new theme, called a Subordinate Theme. In the eighteenth century there was generally little difference in the mood or spirit between the main and subordinate themes. When there is a marked contrast in these themes—a main theme, bold, arresting, and a subordinate theme, lyric, tender, like the hero and heroine of a drama—it is a product generally found in the sonatas and symphonies not of eighteenth-century but of nineteenth-century composers. To bridge the gap from the first to the second tonal level a modulatory section is needed to move the music smoothly from one key to another. This is called an Episode. In the eighteenth century, especially in first and last movements utilizing sonata-form, the episode was an animated, bustling section in the spirit of Italian comic opera. To round out the exposition a small coda or codetta is affixed to bring this portion to a graceful close on the second tonal level. Sometimes the material of the codetta takes on distinct thematic characteristics and may be called a Closing Theme. Or there may be a succession of thematic ideas as we so often find in Mozart, in which this codetta is termed a Closing Section. Charted out then the exposition looks like this:

Main Theme	Episode	Subordinate Theme	Closing Theme or Section
Tonic	Modulatory	Dominant	Dominant

Usually there is a sign at the end indicating that the whole exposition is to be repeated.

The development section generally presents the thematic material of the exposition under varying circumstances. These may include placing the material in new, remote keys, fragmentizing themes and using the fragments in sequence, or, largely in the Classical period, utilizing contrapuntal devices. It is not unusual for the composer to introduce new motives or themes in the development. He may use any one, a few, or all of the themes in the exposition.

In the recapitulation the composer restates the material of the exposition in the order in which it originally appeared. Since the subordinate and closing themes will now be in the tonic key, the function of the episode is different. It is not unusual to find it omitted entirely.

Sometimes the composer feels that a more conclusive ending to the movement is needed and will affix a coda (literally, a tail piece). The coda does not alter the original design but is merely an appendage. The same mood or spirit pervades consistently throughout the movement.

The nomenclature in music is the most confusing of any art. A term used in one century to define a certain type of music may, in the next century, be used to define something entirely different. Or a term used in one country may mean one thing and in another country something else. Even in our own time one school of thought may use one set of terms and another school, describing the same thing, may come up with a completely different nomenclature. Hence confusion exists between "sonata" and "sonata-form." The term *sonata* was used to describe a kind of instrumental music as early as the sixteenth century. It simply means "sounding piece" and is no more definite than that. During the seventeenth century some pieces designated as sonatas were pieces in one movement but divisible into several brief sections of contrasting style. Toward the end of the century such a sonata was found to have the sections reduced in number and even detached from each other to form separate movements. The term "movement" refers largely to tempo. The movements in these sonatas often alternated between fast and slow tempos. They "move" at varying speeds. With the number of movements reduced, each movement in turn was expanded in length. The number of movements varied, four being the norm in the usual church sonata, and were arranged in an order like this: Slow—Fast—Slow—Fast. This is the plan we usually find in the sonatas of Bach and Handel.

We are concerned with the sonata in the Rococo period. The preferred type was the one written for a solo instrument with the accompaniment of a harpsichord and usually cast in three movements: Fast—Slow—Fast. A composer like Giuseppe Tartini (1692-1770) in Italy wrote a great many for violin and keyboard. The movements, whether fast or slow, generally follow the two-part plan that has been outlined. While such sonatas are found in abundance, it must be realized too that many were written for solo keyboard. The flowering keyboard sonata generally presented the single-line melody in the right hand and a rather thin-textured harmonic accompaniment in the left hand. This accompaniment might take an arpeggiated form, referred to as "Italian style," like this:

or a form in which the chord is reduced to a pattern called the "Alberti bass," named after an obscure eighteenth-century composer, Domenico Alberti, like this:

In the Rococo period melody is usually short-breathed. In the Classic period the melody generally embraces a series of balanced phrases and will often seem folk-like in style.

Among the many composers of keyboard sonatas in the Rococo, these should be singled out as significant: Carl Philipp Emanuel Bach (1714-1788), Johann Schobert (1720-1767), Padre Antonio Soler (1729-1783), and Johann Christian Bach (1735-1782). Of these the greatest is C.P.E. Bach who composed over one hundred which exhibit an unusual skill, invention, and originality. Bach goes beyond his contemporaries in the wider range of emotions he conveys. This expressiveness was defined by the Germans as *empfindsamer Stil* or sensitive style. Instead of a single mood sustained throughout the movement, this composer, probably the most talented of Bach's sons, is likely to present a variety of moods from the boisterous to the languid. Most of the sonatas are cast in a three-movement plan which became the norm for keyboard sonatas. Throughout the eighteenth century there was considerable discussion and writing on the subject of expressiveness in instrumental music. C.P.E. Bach, even with the absence of words to guide him in formulating musical ideas, showed the way toward creating definite moods in pure instrumental music and furthermore communicated these moods to the listener. Of course we must realize that the eighteenth century had to conform to a certain code of decorum and controlled excesses of emotion in art and even in their daily lives. It will take a new period, the uninhibited nineteenth century, to overflow with emotional feeling. The eighteenth century exhibited a certain poise and restraint and kept its emotions under control.

As time progressed, composers of the eighteenth century began to entertain more variety in their choice of design for movements. The first movement was invariably in sonata-form. But the second movement, although often in sonata-form, might take on the A B A plan of the opera aria or might even be in theme-and-variation plan. Much of this same flexibility was applied to the last movement as well. Again the prevalent design is the sonata-form, but the rondo, an expansion of the A B A design, is also found, especially in Mozart. Quite simply we have a statement of material, a digression, a return to the first statement, a second digression, and a final restatement of the initial material. Using letters to designate the material we have A B A C A. Other forms too were used, including some hybrid designs.

The apogee of the Classical style is reached in the sonatas of Muzio Clementi (1752-1832), Haydn, Mozart, and Beethoven. Franz Joseph Haydn (1732-1809) modeled many of his 50 sonatas on those of C.P.E. Bach. Mozart, however, is the more universal composer. His ability to embrace the best of all styles prevalent in the eighteenth century is revealed in his 21 sonatas for keyboard. No doubt the unique advantages Mozart enjoyed as a traveling virtuoso and his wide acquaintance with the music of his own period as well as that of J.S. Bach and Handel resulted in this universality.

Ludwig van Beethoven (1770-1827) was the most important contributor to the sonata in the history of music. Of his 600 works, one-fourth belongs in the sonata category. The piano sonatas alone span forty years of his life, from 1782 until 1822. The sonatas of Haydn and Mozart, along with those of C.P.E. Bach and Clementi, served as models for Beethoven. Unlike Haydn's and Mozart's sonatas, however, Beethoven's rank among his best works. He was also more successful than either of his predecessors in getting his sonatas published.

Beethoven's first sonata for piano was written when he was eleven, no doubt with the aid of his teacher, Christian Gottlob Neefe (1748-1798). The three sonatas constituting Opus 2 with which most editions of his piano sonatas begin today were dedicated to Haydn with whom he studied for a brief time. But it was with the "Pathétique," "Moonlight," "Waldstein," and "Appassionata" sonatas that Beethoven's reputation soared. These works brought a new note of expression into pianoforte music hitherto unrealized. Typical of the rising Romantic era, all kinds of programmatic elements were read into these sonatas, even by Beethoven himself.

The "Waldstein," Op. 53 (1803-1804), so called from its dedication to Count von Waldstein, shows the advantage Beethoven took of the rapidly rising mechanical improvements being made on the piano. Before composing the Sonata, Opus 106, he considered the "Appassionata," Opus 57 (1804-1805), to be his greatest sonata.

The last five sonatas, commencing with Opus 101, left Beethoven's devotees in a quandary and prompted his critics to make hostile remarks. They led his listeners into uncharted techniques, forms, and styles. His followers turned to the only means available to them: romanticized, poetic interpretations. The Sonata in B-flat major, Opus 106, known as the "Hammerklavier" Sonata (1816-1818), is the longest of any of Beethoven's sonatas, the most difficult technically, and, for the audiences of his time, the most difficult to comprehend. The composer worked for a year and a half on it and declared it to be his greatest.

In addition to the piano sonatas, written in three, four, or, as in Opus 111, in two movements, Beethoven also wrote 10 sonatas for violin and piano and 5 sonatas for cello and piano. Strangely enough the sonata was not a popular medium of musical expression at public concerts. Only one, possibly Opus 90 in E minor, scholars are not certain, was ever played in a public concert during Beethoven's lifetime.

It must be kept in mind that sonatas were written for every media, as keyboard solos, as pieces for one or two solo instruments with keyboard accompaniment, and even for ensembles of instruments. They supplied students with study material, amateurs with diversions, and professional virtuosi with a repertoire for private and public concerts.

One other type of keyboard piece popular in the eighteenth century should be mentioned. This is the *Fantasy* which, as its name implies, was a rhapsodic composition whose form was usually sectional, each section being strongly contrasted with its neighbor. However, in the Classic period it is not unusual to find Fantasies whose design closely resembles the sonata-form.

SUPPLEMENTARY READING

Einstein. *Mozart: His Character, His Work*. pp. 237-251.
Grout. *A History of Western Music*. pp. 411-426; 470-471.
Landon & Mitchell. *The Mozart Companion*. pp. 32-64.
Láng. *Music in Western Civilization*. pp. 591-603.
Ulrich & Pisk. *A History of Music and Musical Style*. pp. 312-325.

It is urged too that William S. Newman's book on the *Sonata in the Classic Era* be perused for its wealth of reference material.

SUGGESTED LISTENING

The ready availability of the music and recordings of keyboard sonatas by C.P.E. Bach, Haydn, Mozart, and Beethoven makes it difficult to single out any one or two selections. Among the best of Bach are the six "Prussian" sonatas (1742) and six "Würtemberg" sonatas (1744) on which both Haydn and Mozart based their style.

THE CONCERTO

Besides hundreds of sonatas for solo keyboard and for an instrument with keyboard accompaniment composers favored another medium of expression, the concerto, a work for solo instrument accompanied by the orchestra. With the rise of virtuosity and the desire on the part of listeners to enjoy a brilliant display of technique on an instrument, just as they did of the vocalists in the opera house, the solo concerto became a favorite. Developed late in the seventeenth century by Torelli and especially Vivaldi, the concerto was one of the first types of music to rid itself of many Baroque devices of counterpoint. Once freed from polyphonic restrictions the way was cleared for the introduction of idiomatic figurations for the solo instrument. The resultant style was more in keeping with the progressive tendencies leading to the Rococo and Classic eras. In its exterior plan the concerto was cast in three movements: Fast—Slow—Fast. The plan has remained quite consistent up to the present day. In its interior design the first and last movements were cast in what has been termed *ritornello* form, or, more correctly, *ritornello* style. This term had been used in opera to refer to the orchestral introductions, closes, or interludes in arias. So when in the concerto we have similar sections given to the orchestra, they are referred to as *ritornelli.* The first movement of a concerto in this period alternated between the orchestra (called *tutti*) and the soloist, each section being in an appropriate key similar to the sonata. Charted out it looks like this:

TUTTI[1]	SOLO[1]	TUTTI[2]	SOLO[2]	TUTTI[3]	SOLO[3]	TUTTI[4]
Statement of motives in tonic key.	Material drawn from the ritornello or new motives. Tonic— Dominant	Dominant key.	May have new motives. Modulatory.	Relative minor key.	Modulatory but more toward tonic. Possibly a cadenza.	Tonic. Repeat of material from first ritornello.

The thematic material is made up of brief musical figures or motives, not long-breathed melodies as one is likely to find in a nineteenth-century concerto. The plan of the movement can be extended to include another solo section (SOLO[4]) and ritornello (TUTTI[5]), but the chart describes the norm. The composer may utilize in the solo sections material stated in the opening ritornello, or he may present entirely new material in each of the three sections in which the soloist is featured. The tutti, however, will almost consistently use the same thematic material. When the soloist plays, the orchestra drops out in favor of a thin accompaniment of harpsichord reinforced by a cello. Thus the soloist need not strain to be heard above the orchestra. Occasionally the orchestra will interrupt the soloist to insert a motive of its own in the solo section. Before the final ritornello the soloist was often obliged to play a cadenza, that free, unbarred device used to display further the technical prowess of the soloist. It was derived from the opera aria and could be improvised by the performer on the spot, thus displaying another facet of his skill, or it could be prepared in advance.

Strangely enough the ritornello plan continued on through the course of the eighteenth century. Many concertos of Tartini and C.P.E. Bach follow the plan implicitly. Even the first movements of many concertos of Mozart must be approached in analysis by this method. However, the invention and universal acceptance of the sonata-form exerted its influence on the concerto. Hence the "classical" concerto begins with a tutti that often resembles the exposition of a sonata. There follows a repeat of the material by the soloist. Here again composers are not consistent. Mozart may do as Vivaldi frequently did and present new material. Tutti[2] and Solo[2] take on the features of the sonata development section, and Tutti[3] and Solo[3] assume the function of the recapitulation. There is the same use of the cadenza, and Tutti[4] is like a coda. Even the key relationships of of the Vivaldi concerto remain much the same in the Classic concerto concept.

The design of the slow movement varied from concerto to concerto. It may consist of a simple harmonic interlude connecting the two outer movements to a song-like, extended aria. Concertos were written for almost every instrument. Since the Italians did not favor winds, most concertos by Italian composers featured the violin. But in Germany we are likely to find concertos for wind instruments as well as concertos for string or keyboard instruments.

SUPPLEMENTARY READING

Einstein. *Mozart: His Character, His Work.* pp. 287-315.
Landon & Mitchell. *The Mozart Companion.* pp. 200-279.

SUGGESTED LISTENING

Among the best of Mozart's keyboard concertos, and the choice is difficult, is No. 24 in C minor (K.491). Of Beethoven's, No. 4 in G major, Op. 58, and No. 5 in E-flat major ("Emperor"), Op. 73, are among the best, and of course one of the most famous violin concertos ever composed, the Concerto in D major, Op. 61. More difficult to obtain in both music and recordings are concertos by C.P.E. and Johann Christian Bach but no less important in a study of the evolution of this medium.

THE DIVERTIMENTO

Among compositions for chamber groups on the Rococo and Classic periods was the *divertimento*. This is the generic term which embraces similar types sometimes called cassation, serenade, notturno, to name a few. But all utilize an ensemble of strings or winds or mixed groups of strings and winds, generally with one or two players to the part. By and large the divertimento served as music for outdoor entertainment, largely as background music. Since it was frequently performed out of doors, the harpsichord could be excluded. This necessitated creating an instrumentation in which the harmony was adequately filled in by such instruments as horns or violas, thus taking over a function which had been the prerogative of the harpsichord. The number of movements in a divertimento varies from four to ten and are relatively short. However, the norm is five and is arranged as follows:

First Movement: Fast. Second Movement: Minuet. Third Movement: Slow. Fourth Movement: Minuet. Fifth Movement: Fast.

The first movement assumes the aspect of sonata-form; the second and fourth are dances, generally minuets; the third, the slow movement, is song-like. The final movement may have sonata-form quality, but a favorite type was the theme and variation. Generally the element of color was stressed in which each variation in turn featured a different instrument as soloist. This was especially true in ensembles of wind instruments or mixed ensembles of winds and strings.

SUPPLEMENTARY READING
Einstein. *Mozart: His Character, His Work.* pp. 196-214.
Landon & Mitchell. *The Mozart Companion.* pp. 66-89.

THE STRING QUARTET

One is likely to consider the string quartet as the aristocrat of chamber music. And indeed it is. But a great deal of experimentation and trial and error in musical composition had to be carried on before we reach the point in the eighteenth century when a chamber ensemble of four stringed instruments was considered the ideal. Examples of the use of two violins, a viola, and a cello for an ensemble can be found early in the century, but these examples are in a style foreign to our concept of string quartet music. Until each instrument had some independence and could on occasion carry the melodic motives in its own part, we do not have genuine string quartet writing. Even the early works of Haydn give the first violin almost exclusive rights to the melody, with the inner parts duplicating the melody in octaves or accompanying in intervals of thirds or sixths. Indeed it seems necessary to utilize the harpsichord to fill out the harmonies and duplicate the cello part as bass. The aim then of the quartet composer was to get cohesion in his medium, emancipating the viola from its slavish duplication of the cello part and allowing each instrument to manipulate at some time the basic thematic material.

Among the first of the successful experimenters with the string quartet was Luigi Boccherini (1743-1805), an Italian who made his reputation as a performer and composer, not in his native land, but in France, Spain, and Prussia, the first six of whose 102 quartets were published in Paris in 1761 as Opus 1. These works already show tendencies of real string quartet writing described above. The independence of parts does not lean on fugal writing but in interchange of the parts in a homophonic texture. Thus at times the cello may carry the melody, while the second violin may play, in its range, the part normally allotted to the bass. Typical of what his conferees were doing in Italy, Boccherini cast his quartets in three movements, often with the last a minuet.

The composer who did more than any other to create the real quartet style was Joseph Haydn and one may trace the whole evolution of its development in over 80 of his quartets. One of the first positions Haydn held was in the household of Baron Karl Joseph von Fürnberg whose country estate was at Weinzierl in Lower Austria. The baron found great enjoyment in chamber music and arranged for almost daily concerts with an ensemble that included Haydn, then about 20 years of age, as the first violinist. According to one of Haydn's early biographers, Giuseppe Carpani, it was the baron who urged Haydn to try his hand at writing string quartets. Haydn had written some string trios, a good stepping-stone to quartet writing, and now experimented with this new medium. He wrote about 18 for the baron, calling them not quartets but divertimenti. They were generally written in five movements with two minuets, which we found to be characteristic of the divertimento. They exhibited all the characteristics of typical Rococo writing—a clearly-defined melodic line given to the first violin and a simple harmonic background relegated to the other strings.

When Haydn accepted a position with the powerful Eszterházy family in Hungary in 1761, it was not long before he turned his attention once again to the string quartet. One senses that the composer was struggling to create a style compatible with these four instruments. To give independence to each part he turned, in his Opus 20 (1772), to a Baroque technique, the fugue, which he utilized in the last movement of these four-movement pieces. One senses too the frustration Haydn must have experienced in trying to solve the problem of string quartet writing. From 1772 to 1781 he abandoned the medium. This is something of a dramatic moment in music history.

Mozart wrote his first quartet at the age of 14, and, like Haydn's early efforts, it is not a real quartet. Originally written in three movements, with a fourth added later, it shows marked Italian influence.

The 12 quartets which he wrote in 1772 and 1773 indicate that Mozart found himself in much the same position with respect to style as Haydn. Mozart familiarized himself with the Haydn quartets and turned likewise to the fugue which we find in the finales of K.168 and 173. No doubt Mozart was confused by Haydn as Haydn was himself confused. For ten years, from 1773 to 1783, a very long time in Mozart's brief career, he did not write any more string quartets.

Then came Haydn's Opus 33, the six "Russian" quartets of 1781, which seemed at last to solve the problem of writing for this medium. The composer in submitting these quartets to his publisher Artaria in Vienna emphasized the fact that they were written "in an entirely new and special manner," as indeed they are. The thematic material is motivic, and the motives are shared alike by all the instruments and worked through the parts polyphonically, with the motive not juxtaposed but kneaded into the texture. Thus Haydn was on the way to creating some of his greatest masterpieces in this literature. It should be pointed out that what is unique about Haydn's quartets is the fact that despite their superb artistic quality, the technical demands on the performers are not too great. Not Mozart and certainly not Beethoven can claim such a distinguished attribute. During the course of the nineteenth and twentieth centuries the burden of technical problems posed by composers for the performers of string quartets increased.

Haydn's quartets, Op. 33, made a profound impression on Mozart. After a careful study of them he proceeded to write the six quartets which form his Opus 10. Mozart dedicated them to Haydn, and they have been referred to as the "Haydn" Quartets. The history of music has seldom seen among its composers the high regard and mutual respect Haydn and Mozart had for each other, personally and professionally. Like Haydn's quartets, all four instruments of Opus 10 share in the musical discourse with thematic development. Mozart wrote only four quartets after the "Haydn" Quartets, the "Hoffmeister" (K.499) and the three "Prussian" Quartets (K.575, 589, 590), but they are among the greatest in the literature. Four is the normal number of movements for both Haydn's and Mozart's quartets.

Toward the turn of the century another voice is heard, that of Beethoven. Between 1798 and 1800 he wrote his first quartets, Opus 18. The six quartets which constitute this opus are often called the "Lobkovitz" Quartets after the prince to whom they are dedicated. The style and character of these pieces owe much to Haydn and Mozart. There are unexpected turns, humorous thrusts, and often a tender lyricism which points the way toward Beethoven's later efforts in this medium. Like

Haydn's quartets, these are not too demanding on the players. Beethoven wrote them for four talented teen-age boys who used to play every Friday morning at Prince Lichnowsky's castle in Vienna. The prince was so pleased with the quartets that he settled a generous annuity on Beethoven.

With the development of new compositional techniques and changes in taste and style, a new chapter in string quartet writing emerged in the next period of Beethoven's life. Between the Opus 18 Quartets and the emergence of the "Rasoumovsky" Quartets, Opus 59, the composer had grown in wisdom and artistic stature. The wealth and depth of musical ideas, the brilliant effects, and the almost orchestral variety and power initiated a new concept of string quartet writing.

Count Rasoumovsky, the Russian Ambassador to Austria, made his luxurious palace in Vienna a center of musical life. The Count commissioned Beethoven to write three quartets for him which Beethoven completed around the first of the year in 1807. There is evidence that whenever they were first played, whether in Vienna, Moscow, or London, they met with adverse criticism by performers and audiences alike. They were technically difficult for the players, and the emotional content of the music was more than the listeners, seeped as they were in Classic traditions, could tolerate. Like the twentieth-century audience listening to a new composition embracing serial techniques or electronic devices, the early nineteenth-century audience reacted with, "Is this music?"

The three quartets of Opus 59, No. 1 in F major, No. 2 in E minor, and No. 3 ("Hero") in C major, use orchestral effects of sonority which were to become a characteristic of string quartets generally in the nineteenth century. The F major Quartet has the unique distinction of having each of its four movements cast in sonata-form, even the scherzo movement. In the finale of the mighty C major Quartet Beethoven uses the fugue to create tension and climax. Indeed fugues or fugue-like passages run through many of his greatest works, generally for climactic purposes.

Between the Quartets of Opus 59 and the last five which Beethoven wrote are two: the "Harp" in E-flat major, Opus 74 (1809), and the "Quartett Serioso" in F minor, Opus 95 (1810). Although separated by only a year there is a wide contrast of style between the two. The "Harp" consists of four autonomous movements; the "Quartett Serioso" is unified in its movements through thematic repetition. Unlike the Quartets of Opus 59, Opus 95 avoids the orchestral style and is more intimate. The formal structure is clear, the movements short and concentrated.

The last quartets of Beethoven, written between 1824 and 1826, rather defy a clear-cut period classification. Aside from the increased number of movements which reflects a return to the eighteenth-century divertimento, there is nothing of the Classic era about them. Beethoven would not be confined to the limits of a prescribed design but would modify old forms and even invent new ones.

Three of the quartets, Opus 127 in E-flat major ("La gaieté"), Opus 130 in B-flat major ("Quartetto Scherzoso"), and Opus 132 in A minor were commissioned by Prince Galitzin, another Russian enthusiast of chamber music. Two other quartets belong in this last group of five: the Quartet in C-sharp minor, Opus 131, and Beethoven's last work in this medium, the Quartet in F major, Opus 135. So concentrated is the material in these works, so abstruse the contents that they have never been especially popular with any but the most ardent devotees. They are, however, among the great masterpieces of quartet literature. Within a few short years Beethoven made giant strides, taking a medium that was comparatively new and making of it a musical form that has served as a model for composers for generations.

OTHER CHAMBER MUSIC

Because of the homogeneity of its medium, the string quartet is held to be the ideal type of chamber music. However it should not be deemed to be the only type. Composers often experimented with larger ensembles, sometimes mixing winds with strings. The string quartet in the hands of Haydn, Mozart, and Beethoven pointed the way toward making each instrument an integral part of the musical fabric. Whatever instruments were used in combination, each had to carry equal responsibility in a basically homophonic texture overlaid with polyphonic devices.

Among the more famous quartets with wind instruments are those of Mozart. Three flute quartets (flute, violin, viola, and cello), K.285, 285a, and Anh.171, were commissioned in 1777 by a rich Dutch amateur, Monsieur de Jean, then residing in Mannheim. A fourth flute quartet (K.298) was written in Paris. These can't begin to compare in quality with the quartet for oboe and strings (K.370) which Mozart wrote for the celebrated German oboist, Friedrich Ramm, in Munich early in 1781.

When the piano was introduced into the ensemble after the dissolution of the *basso continuo* system, new problems beset composers. The piano, with its capacity to play many parts at once, seemed to impose itself on the other instruments and endanger the balance which had been so skillfully achieved in chamber music without keyboard. Unlike the harpsichord, the tone quality of the piano did not blend well with the strings. Therefore when the piano was utilized, a different approach to chamber music was taken. The piano is liable to assume the role of contender, to be pitted against the other instruments of the ensemble rather than to blend with them.

One of the great pieces of chamber music by Mozart is the Piano Quartet in G minor (K.478) which the composer wrote early in 1786. The demands on the pianist are severe, equal certainly to what Mozart would expect of a pianist in a piano concerto. The string parts too (violin, viola, cello) have that integration of thematic texture one has come to expect from the late string quartets of the master, but this Piano Quartet goes further. Contrary to the general attitude of the eighteenth century that music should serve a sociable purpose, to be listened to superficially and with a smile, this work has passion, depth, and an earnestness about it that hints of things to come in the next century. Its companion piece, the Piano Quartet in E-flat major (K.493), was completed a few months later. Because of the criticism launched by the publisher against the G minor Quartet, that it was too difficult to attract prospective buyers, Mozart made this one a little easier technically. It is bright and original with only a hint of menacing, darker shades. Both quartets are cast in three movements.

In addition to trios and quartets for either strings alone or in combination with winds, there are many examples of quintets. String quintets differ little from string quartets. Usually the additional part is given to a second viola. Between 1787 and 1791 Mozart composed four string quintets, intending to dedicate them to the new king of Prussia, Frederick William II, a violoncello-playing dilettante. Evidently Mozart planned to write a set of six for this purpose, but the dedication never came off. He completed the quintets K.515 and 516. Then Johann Tost, a wealthy Hungarian merchant and apt violinist, commissioned Mozart to write some chamber music for him. Mozart again turned to the medium of the string quintet and wrote two, K.593 in D major and K.614 in E-flat major. These works, like the string quartets, are cast in four movements and contain some of the most sublime music Mozart ever composed. One other quintet should be mentioned here, the so-called Stadler Quintet, K.581 (1789), for clarinet and string quartet. Like the oboe quartet in which the oboe assumes the role normally designated to the first violin in a string quartet, the clarinet takes the leading part. At the same time there is a wonderful confraternity between the wind instrument and its string cousins.

Beethoven wrote only one string quintet, this in C major and published as Opus 29 in 1802. Although it does not come up to the standard we expect from the master of some of the greatest quartet literature, it does have a certain charm.

When Mozart completed his Quintet in E-flat major for Oboe, Clarinet, Bassoon, Horn, and Piano (K.452), he wrote a letter to his father, dated April 10, 1784, saying, "I myself consider [this Quintet] . . . to be the best work I have ever composed." Mozart's skill in understanding the potentialities of each of the instruments and in maintaining their individuality makes for a superb example of artistic craftsmanship. In 1797 Beethoven tried his hand with the same combination but with far less success.

SUPPLEMENTARY READING

Einstein. *Mozart: His Character, His Work*. pp. 167-195.
Landon & Mitchell. *The Mozart Companion*. pp. 90-137.

SUGGESTED LISTENING

The complete quartets of Haydn, Mozart, and Beethoven are readily available on records. Any of the quartets that go to make up Haydn's Opus 76 are worthy of study, particularly No. 3, the "Emperor." Of Mozart's the six quartets which constitute Opus 10, the so-called "Haydn" Quartets, or the composer's last three quartets, the "Prussian," are among his greatest.

Included in the best chamber music other than the string quartet are Mozart's Quartet for Oboe and Strings and the great Piano Quartet in G minor.

THE SYMPHONY

The evolution and early development of the symphony in the eighteenth century is still shrouded in mystery, but let it be understood at once that credit for its origin cannot be attributed to any one man, any one school, or even to any one nation. It was one of those forms that seems to have arisen almost simultaneously everywhere. By definition we understand the term symphony to be a composition for orchestra divisible into movements—three or four—of varying tempos. Like other instrumental media, the first symphonies were designed to be entertaining and were largely frivolous or at least cheerful compositions, serving largely as musical background for social functions. For what it is worth, of over 7,000 symphonies listed in the *Union Thematic Catalog of Eighteenth-Century Symphonies,* only about 140 or 2% are in a minor key, and half of these are by French composers. This percentage might be a reasonable estimate for solo sonatas as well. However, by the end of the century many symphonies were serious or at least very expressive works of art. From this time on in the history of music the symphony has become the product of the composer's most profound musical thought and often of his highest artistic achievement.

Seldom in the course of the eighteenth century did a symphony, as it does today, occupy the central position on a program, even in public concerts. Usually the movements were broken up to allow other musical fare to come to the fore. Hence the first three movements of a symphony might be played followed by a concerto or possibly an operatic aria or two and then the last movement of the symphony.

Let us try to trace now the sources of style for the eighteenth-century symphony. First there are the *external,* those sources which have to do with the over-all plan of the symphony. These spring from two Baroque sources of the early eighteenth century: (1) the Italian opera overture or sinfonia; (2) the Baroque sonata. The overture in Italian opera, as previously mentioned, served no other purpose than to summon the audience to its seats. It was generally cast in three sections: Fast–Slow–Fast. When a nobleman had at his disposal an orchestra to entertain him in his chambers, he often requested of the orchestra the performance of one of these overtures which he had heard at the opera house. So when we lift this overture from the opera house pit and place it in the chamber or concert room, the first step in the creation of the sinfonia as an independent concert piece has been taken.

The Baroque sonata of the early eighteenth century was an amalgamation of the church sonata and the chamber sonata of the seventeenth century. The church sonata consisted of four abstract movements arranged as Slow–Fast–Slow–Fast. The chamber sonata was made up of a series of idealized dances, like the keyboard suite. Toward the close of the seventeenth century the chamber sonata began to borrow one or two abstract movements from the church sonata. This is evident in the use of the term Prelude for the initial movement of a suite of dances. The church sonata (so called because it was actually performed during the church service) borrowed now and then a dance or dance-like movement from the chamber sonata, generally for the last movement. The borrowings continued into the eighteenth century until no real line of demarcation between church and chamber sonata is distinguishable. However, it seems plausible that the slow introduction to many symphonies, notably those of Haydn, sprang from the plan of the church sonata. Likewise the use of the minuet in many symphonies undoubtedly originated from the chamber sonata.

The *internal* sources of style have to do with the plan or structure, the texture, the mood, and key relationships of individual movements. These are not as easy to trace as the external sources. We have already described the two-part sonata-form and its expansion to include a distinct development section. This is the design composers were most likely to adopt as the first movement. But we should not minimize the importance of the ritornello form as used in the solo concerto, especially in its basically three-part structure and more particularly in its key relationships. Texture too plays a significant role. Where in the solo concerto the orchestral tutti initiates the thematic material, we have, in the symphony movement, the announcement of the main theme. When the solo instrument enters in the ritornello form at a subdued dynamic level, we have something comparable to the subordinate theme area. During the Rococo period music was played largely in what has been described as "terrace" dynamics—the music was either played loud or soft with little gradation between. Experiments in *crescendo* (increased loudness) and *diminuendo* (decreased loudness) which had been carried out in the early years of the eighteenth century were for a time abandoned, not to return again until the Classic period. The concept of having the full orchestra play and then thinning out to areas where only a few instruments are involved stems too from the *concerto grosso* (literally, large ensemble), one of the most important and popular types of chamber music of the late seventeenth and early eighteenth centuries. Here a large group of instruments (*concerto* or *ripieno*) is pitted against a smaller group (the *concertino,* or little ensemble). Arcangelo Corelli (1653-1713) was largely responsible for its invention and was imitated, among others, by Handel, Geminiani, and J.S. Bach (Brandenburg Concertos). The alternation of the solo group with the full orchestra might be compared to an embossed fabric like brocade.

The general, over-all spirit of gaiety and excitement in the first and last movements of symphonies is drawn from the Italian comic opera with its patter songs and bustling, nervous energy. The slow movements, often lyrical and subdued, take their form and style from arias stemming from both comic and serious opera.

We mentioned that no one country is responsible for the development of the symphony. Yet for practical purposes we must begin somewhere. Italy seems to be as good a place as any. And with respect to time, the second generation of eighteenth-century composers seems the most reasonable, the year around 1740. Italian composers are likely to adhere to the three-movement plan with the third movement a dance, more particularly a minuet. Italian symphonies especially are imbued with the spirit of the comic opera with a slow movement that is seldom serious but which may take on the aspects of a serenade. One of the earliest and most significant of the early symphonists was Giovanni Battista Sammartini (1700/01-1775), a teacher of Gluck. In one of his symphonies for strings, dated about 1744, the first movement already has all the ingredients of a clearly-defined sonata-form with the divisions of almost equal length: an exposition of 17 measures, a development section of 16 measures, and a recapitulation of 17 measures. Since sonata-form is dependent on key relationship and since the whole concept of functional harmony as we know it today was comparatively new at this time, it was necessary for the composer to orient the listener from the start with the key of the tonic. This Sammartini did with a main theme consisting of chords in the violins and the G major scale played in the lower strings.

Sammartini: Sinfonia in G major for Strings, 1st movement

Sammartini's 77 symphonies show him to be a cut above his Italian contemporaries in this medium. They play a significant role in the transition from Baroque to Classic forms, textures, and procedures. The symphonies follow closely the three-movement plan, utilize the two- and three-part sonata-form, and show clarity, integration, and developmental devices unique for the time. They have rhythmic drive and a wider range of expression than one might encounter from composers at this time.

Other Italian symphonists include Baldassare Galuppi (1706-1785), Niccolò Jommelli, and later, Luigi Boccherini and Giovanni Cambini (1746-1825).

Another school, greatly influenced by the Italians and in turn one of the most influential in western Europe, was the Bohemian. One of the earliest composers of symphonies was Václav Míča (1694-1744), the conductor of Count Questenberg's orchestra at Jaroměřice in southwest Moravia. One of his symphonies, in D major, was written about 1740. Because of its advanced techniques in form and orchestration, it was long thought to be a product of Míča's son a generation later. However, Czechoslovakian musicologists proved that the elder Míča had access to Italian scores that revealed clear-cut sonata-form. The Symphony in D, like the Italian symphonies, is in three movements. The final movement is marked *Fuga* and combines the imitative character of the fugue with the sonata-form. The main theme is a complete fugal exposition in gigue style. It is doubtful that Míča's son, a generation later, would have ever considered using contrapuntal techniques like these. Míča senior was still close to the Baroque era. The instrumentation includes 2 oboes, 2 horns, 2 trumpets, timpani, and strings.

Most native-born Bohemian composers made their reputations elsewhere in Europe, but the importance of this school, long neglected by scholars, cannot be overestimated. Included are Franz Xaver Pokorny (1728-1794), Leopold Florian Gassmann (1729-1774), Joseph Mysliweczek (1737-1781), and Franz Anton Rösler (Antonio Rosetti, 1750-1792).

Vienna in the eighteenth century was the hub of the musical universe —the melting pot of musical Europe. It maintained close contact with Italy, was linked with other "German" schools, but contributed many original ideas of its own. Perhaps the best-known Viennese composer at the beginning of the century was Johann Joseph Fux (1660-1741), the Kapellmeister of the Imperial Court. He is best remembered today as the author of the most influential treatise on counterpoint in the eighteenth century: *Gradus ad Parnassum* (published originally in Latin; Vienna, 1725).

With the death of Charles VI in 1740 a new spirit began to permeate Austria. His daughter, Maria Theresa (1717-1780), succeeded him, and a new generation of young, progressive composers began to control the musical life of Vienna. Men like Georg Matthias Monn (1717-1750) and Georg Christoph Wagenseil (1715-1777) wrote symphonies largely in the Italian spirit. Wagenseil's are in three movements, usually ending with a minuet. In his Symphony in D major (1746) the minuet is cast in an embryonic sonata-form. Monn is best remembered for writing symphonies in four movements which include a minuet as either the second or third movement. By the 1760's Viennese composers were to accept the four-movement plan as the norm. In the sonata-form itself one is likely to find each section, exposition, development, recapitulation, of equal length. The Viennese too paid more attention to the development section than we find in other schools in the mid-century. The school reached its apogee in the symphonies of Haydn, Mozart, and Beethoven.

Perhaps the best known of all these schools is that of Mannheim. The Elector Palatine in Mannheim was Duke Theodor (1724-1799) who made his city in southwest Germany one of the greatest cultural centers. Among his most important achievements was the establishment of a court orchestra made up of Italian, Austrian, and Bohemian musicians. There were 12 violins, 2 violas, 2 cellos, 3 basses, 15 wind instruments available, and timpani. Later the orchestra was expanded to include 22 violins, 4 violas, 4 cellos, 2 basses, winds in pairs, and timpani. As the leader of this extraordinary group Duke Theodor chose Johann Stamitz (1717-1757), a Bohemian violinist of exceptional talents. Stamitz drilled the musicians to the precision in ensemble he demanded, made the violins use uniform bowing, and insisted the men observe closely the dynamic markings in the music.

Most of the symphonies written by Mannheim composers, who were also members of the orchestra, were cast in four movements with the third a minuet: Fast—Slow—Minuet—Fast. In the first movement, always cast in sonata-form, there was generally an abundance of thematic material. This material was largely motivic in character, for the concept of organizing thematic material into balanced phrases was to be a later development.

Development as such, however, consisted largely in placing the thematic material in new keys and using motives in sequence. When a separate development section appeared, it was generally short, about half the length of the exposition.

Stamitz livened the music with sudden loud and soft accents, and although the idea of terrace dynamics, of contrasting loud and soft, was a basic ingredient of musical style, his originality lay in the unpredictable placement of these sudden changes. Stamitz also developed the orchestral crescendo, beginning a passage softly and gradually increasing the volume. This is said to have made a profound impression on the audiences at Mannheim. Haydn was to adopt this technique, and it has often been referred to as a steamroller or rocket technique.

Among the most famous composers in Mannheim of Stamitz' generation were Franz Xavier Richter (1709-1789), Ignaz Holzbauer (1711-1783), Anton Filtz (c.1730-1760), and Carlo Giuseppe Toëschi (1724-1788). In 1778 the orchestra was moved to Munich, and its influence waned.

In North Germany an excellent musical establishment was created by Frederick the Great. When Frederick became King of Prussia and Elector of Brandenburg in 1740, he had already acquired an orchestra made up of some of the best instrumentalists available: Karl and Johann Graun (Karl was the Kapellmeister), Johann and Franz Benda, violinists, and Johann Quantz, flutist. Later C.P.E. Bach was to join the ensemble and, along with the Grauns, was largely responsible for creating the Berlin style of the symphony. In 1754 the orchestra consisted of 12 violins, 4 violas, 4 cellos, 2 basses, 4 flutes (Frederick himself was a flutist, practiced diligently, played concertos, and often joined the orchestra, and composed), 3 oboes, 4 bassoons, 2 horns, along with viola da gamba, theorbo, and 2 harpsichords to realize the figured bass.

As might be expected, the early group of composers in the North German School wrote in the *style galant*. Unlike their Viennese cousins who were form-conscious symphonists, the North Germans were unconcerned with such intellectual pursuits as thematic transformation or the interplay of tonalities. They were more involved with the expression of passion and pain. Certain terms became associated with their music such as *Affektenlehre*, or the "doctrine of the affections," a kind of catalog of the emotions and their suitable musical expressions. The term *sensibilité*, as understood by the French, meant a formality and restraint which disciplined their art. *Sensibilité*, which became the *Empfindsamer Stil* or *Empfindsamkeit* of the North Germans, took on quite a different meaning. Music became sentimental to the point of being unduly or excessively responsive and expressive.

Of all the composers who wrote symphonies in Berlin, none showed a more intense drive toward individuality than Carl Philipp Emanuel Bach who wrote 18 works in this medium. Bach seemed bent on creating an overall sense of excitement and drama. Look at this theme from his Sinfonia in E minor for Strings (note the minor key) which serves as the main theme of the first movement:

C. P. E. Bach: Sinfonia in E minor for Strings, 1st movement

It is played in unison or octaves by the whole ensemble and exhibits unusual boldness and vigor. Such attempts to stir emotions in the listener initiated a new approach by the composer to the art of music. This approach was to bear fruit in the works of Haydn.

In 1767 Bach obtained a release from his position at the Prussian court, where the routine for more than twenty-five years had become unbearable to him. He succeeded in obtaining an appointment as Kapellmeister in Hamburg, directing the musical functions of the city's five leading churches. Although Bach was largely concerned with sacred music, he did not abandon his secular music activities. His last four symphonies (Wotquenne 183), among his best, were written in 1776. All are in three movements with transitions between the movements. This concept of linking movements as if to form one continuous piece no doubt came from Johann Sebastian Bach's concertos and from the *concerto grosso* of the Baroque period. We will not meet such a conception again in symphonic literature until the nineteenth century.

As in the Sinfonia in E minor, Bach generally writes a fiery unison main theme with which to open his work. There are dramatic changes of key and harmonic intensity in the course of the first movement, tender slow movements with emphasis on orchestral color, and brilliant, meteoric finales. Typical of the North German School, Bach used rhythm and color rather than formal means to achieve his effects and outbursts of passion.

France also had a school of symphonists in the Rococo period, but her influence outside the country was limited. However, France was eager to publish symphonies by German composers, and the fame of Mannheimers such as Stamitz spread more quickly elsewhere in Europe as a result of French publishing than in his native land.

Joseph Haydn wrote over 100 symphonies, a genre of musical expression that occupied his attention from the beginning of his creative life to the end. These symphonies above all his other works reveal his true style: a curious admixture of nervous, aggressive strength combined with a sophisticated poise but through which runs a strong vein of earthy humor. In his youth (1750-1760) he was dependent on the models of other composers, and the result is an amalgamation of some of the best features of the Italian, Viennese, and Mannheim practices. Then between 1760 and 1780 there was a period of transition during which his music became more serious. It is in this period that the influence of C.P.E. Bach and *Empfindsamkeit* are most notable. From 1780, the period of maturity, Haydn exhibited definite Classic tendencies and even an anticipation of the Romantic period. Unlike so many other composers in his time, Haydn seemed to attack the preparation of each symphony with a fresh outlook. Not all of the more than 100 symphonies are masterpieces, but the lesser works always include some interesting features. In 1759 Haydn was engaged as musical director to Count Ferdinand Maximilian von Morzin's musical establishment. Von Morzin had a summer palace at Lukavič in Bohemia and spent the winters in Vienna. The orchestra consisted of 6 violins, 1 viola, 1 bass, 2 oboes, 2 bassoons, and 2 horns. It was for this orchestra that Haydn wrote his first symphony in D major. In casting the work in three movements and maintaining a lively spirit, Haydn showed the influence of the Italians. The development of thematic material and his use of the horns came from the Viennese school. But his use of many themes and the opening orchestral crescendo are definitely Mannheim features. Like his contemporaries Haydn scored the slow movement for strings only.

Thus in the very first symphony we see this amalgamation of styles of which we spoke earlier.

Among the visitors at Lukaveč was Prince Paul Eszterházy, head of one of the most powerful dynasties in Central Europe. When in 1761 reverses of fortune compelled Count Von Morzin to restrict his mode of life and he dismissed his orchestra and its leader, Prince Paul appointed Haydn Vice-Kapellmeister at the Eszterházy estate. The prince, who lived in the Hungarian town of Eisenstadt, was looking for a younger man to assist his aging Kapellmeister, Gregorius Joseph Werner. The orchestra in Eisenstadt consisted of 6 violins, 1 viola, 2 cellos, 2 basses, 1 flute, 2 oboes, 1 bassoon, 2 horns, and 1 pensioned timpani player. Along with Haydn two other distinguished musicians were hired: Luigi Tomasini, a violin virtuoso, and Joseph Weigl, a gifted cellist. Among the first symphonies Haydn wrote for his new orchestra was a set of three, Nos. 6, 7, and 8, bearing the descriptive titles "Morning," "Noon," and "Night," respectively. In these works Haydn wrote extensive solo passages for the newly-engaged virtuosi, thus flattering the members of the orchestra and at the same time producing results which delighted the Prince and his guests. Each of the works is cast in four movements including a minuet. In both No. 6 and No. 7 Haydn for the first time used a slow introduction, a device which he favored in almost all the symphonies of his mature period. Also by organizing his themes into regularly balanced phrases the sonata-form itself gained symmetry, an important feature of the Classic period.

Haydn: Symphony No. 6 in D major, 1st movement

Shortly after he had engaged the services of Haydn, Prince Paul died on March 18, 1762, and was succeeded by his brother, Nikolaus Eszterházy, who loved luxury and display. Then Werner died in 1766, and Haydn became Kapellmeister. One of the first things Prince Nikolaus did was to build a magnificent palace to rival that of Versailles on the site of his hunting lodge not far from Eisenstadt. With an expenditure of about $5 million, the castle of Eszterháza came into existence in 1766. From henceforth Haydn and his musicians were to divide their time between the country estate and Eisenstadt. The orchestra was enlarged, and Haydn was given a free rein to experiment with his instrumental forces. Where his early symphonies emit a kind of joyousness, the works around 1770 take on a seriousness and even bitterness which is not easy to account for. It may have been something in his personal life, or it may have been the overwhelming influence of the music of C.P.E. Bach and Gluck. Among the truly great works of his early maturity are No. 44 in E minor, the so-called "Mourning" Symphony, and No. 45 in F-sharp minor, the "Farewell." Note the use of the minor keys here. Certainly the period from 1763 to 1772 included the most exciting years of Haydn's creative life when his music took on an emotional intensity unique in the eighteenth century. But what was the reaction to the music of this, Haydn's most exciting period, with its breadth of freedom of expression? Prince Nikolaus didn't like it. That powerful thematic material, those bold unisonal passages, the contrapuntal devices Haydn used in the development, those dramatic moments of silence did not please the Prince or his guests.

Haydn's response to his critics was a succession of symphonies from 1774 utilizing his superb technique but wholly lacking in inspiration. We would call it today "commercial" composition, and the great evolution of the art of the symphony came to a standstill. Ironically it is with these uninspired works that Haydn's reputation grew, helped spread his fame throughout Europe, and brought him wealth and honor. However, after 1785 a new spirit permeated his music due in part to his close association with Mozart. Haydn was commissioned to write six symphonies (Nos. 82-87) for Le Concert de la Loge olympique, a Parisian concert organization, and these return again to the wide emotional range of his *Sturm und Drang* period of the previous decade. Many scholars consider these symphonies as approximating the Classical ideal. Le Concert had a much larger orchestra than one would find in Austria or Germany —for example, 40 violins and 10 double basses. Audiences and critics in Paris were ecstatic over the performances, and this reaction encouraged Haydn even more to seek a wider audience than the isolated environment of Eszterháza. He had been in Eisenstadt for nearly thirty years and had outgrown his use for the establishment. On September 28, 1790, Prince Nikolaus died, and Prince Anton, his successor, disbanded the orchestra, retaining a few musicians for the execution of the music for the church services and for the hunt. Haydn was kept on the payroll, but he had no duties to perform. He was granted a leave of absence and went to Vienna to take up residence there. Hearing of this situation, the English impresario, Johann Peter Salomon, approached Haydn with a tempting contract to come to London and conduct performances of his music, including twelve new symphonies which the master was to compose for his London appearances. Haydn accepted the offer, and he and Salomon set out for the arduous journey to London, arriving there on New Year's Day of 1791. No musician in history was treated with such respect and reverence as Haydn was. The nobility vied with each other in arranging receptions and banquets in his honor. He left London in June of 1792 only to return again in January of 1794. The so-called twelve "Salomon" Symphonies (Nos. 93-104) which Haydn wrote expressly for his English audiences, six for the first and six for the second visit, are perhaps the best known of all his works. He was determined to display in them every facet of his knowledge of symphonic composition. Indeed his last symphonies sum up all the practices of symphonic writing up to this time, but in addition they look to the future into a new world that will be created by Beethoven, Schubert, Mendelssohn, and Schumann. Haydn's art is at a consistently high level for all twelve symphonies.

Except for No. 95 all begin with a slow introduction, generally in marked contrast to the spirit of the opening theme of the *Allegro* section. No other composer of his time or before had done so much with the development section of the movements in sonata-form. Here motive is pitted against motive in elaborate contrapuntal techniques. Quick modulations to remote keys and driving rhythmic patterns sustain tension in the listener. The slow movements often retain the variation style prevalent in so many previous works, but there is a tenderness and expressivity in them rivaled only by Mozart. His minuets are no longer merely dances but take on proportions that can only be described as symphonic. The last movements have that wonderful buoyancy and effervescence which is a hallmark of his finales. Haydn experimented with a new design for some of the final movements in his late works— a kind of hybrid combining elements of the sonata and rondo forms. Charted out it looks something like this:

EXPOSITION			MID-SECTION	RECAPITULATION
A	B	A'	C	A
Main Th.	Sub. Th.	Main Th.	New material	Sometimes only the Main Theme appears in the tonic key.
Tonic	Dominant	Tonic		

Coloristically these symphonies are for their time masterpieces of orchestration. The woodwinds are given more freedom, not just duplicating the string parts or decorating the melodic line as is so prevalent in the eighteenth century. Scoring for clarinets appears for the first time in a

Haydn symphony in No. 99. Harmony, however, seems to be the most important element in Haydn's writing and, in these last twelve symphonies, an advance over his previous works. And where chromaticism in the melodic line is an identifying feature in Mozart's music, this chromaticism is an integral part of Haydn's chordal structure.

Five years after Haydn wrote his first symphony, another composer, then only eight years of age, contributed his first efforts to this medium. As might be guessed he was Mozart, and among his forty symphonies are some of the great masterpieces of all times. Perhaps the most influential composer of Mozart's instrumental style was Johann Christian Bach with whom Mozart studied during a brief stay in London in 1764. Later Haydn was to exert his influence on the young composer.

In his early symphonies, elements of the Italian sinfonia and comic opera style are unmistakably evident. They are often cast in a three-movement plan without a minuet, though by the 1760's, as previously mentioned, the Viennese considered four movements the norm. Before long, however, Mozart was to write his symphonies in four movements. The first movement of Symphony No. 1 in E-flat major (K.16) utilizes the two-part sonata design as does the second movement. The third, the final movement, hints at this kind of structure but is something of a hybrid. But even when he uses the normal three-part sonata-form for his first movements, Mozart is likely to make the development section short. This is because he frequently develops his thematic material after its initial appearance in the exposition and consequently, when he reaches the development, has little more he can do with the material. Then too where Haydn invents strong basic motives which lend themselves well to development, Mozart, especially in his later works, will use a vocal type theme in which the development consists largely of the interplay and contrast of the motives.

One of the special features of Mozart's symphonic writing is the delicate coloring he applies. Even in such an early work as No. 20 in D major (K.133) the theme of the slow movement is played in the flute and first violins. The first and second violins are muted, but the lower strings are not. This unusual coloristic device creates an eerie effect.

His journey to Paris and Mannheim in the late 1770's and his acquaintance with Haydn's *Sturm und Drang* symphonies brought about a change in Mozart's style and initiated his second period of writing. In his Symphony No. 31 in D major ("Paris"; K.297), scored for a much larger orchestra than any previous work, we have an assimilation of elements stemming from Mannheim and Vienna.

The last ten years of Mozart's life brought few symphonies, but the six works produced are among the great masterpieces of symphonic literature: No. 35 in D major ("Haffner"; K.385), No. 36 in C major ("Linz"; K.425), No. 38 in D major ("Prague"; K.504), No. 39 in E-flat major (K.543), No. 40 in G minor (K.550), and No. 41 in C major ("Jupiter"; K.551). In the "Linz" Symphony Mozart uses for the first time a slow introduction. And this device is again used in the very next symphony, the "Prague," written between *Figaro* and *Don Giovanni*. This introduction is one of the great expressive sections in the literature, creating unusual tensions for its time.

So much has been written about the last three symphonies, the best-known of Mozart's output, that only a few remarks need be made here. All three were composed in the summer of 1788, but each is quite unique and individual. No. 39 comes closest to being like Haydn. No. 40 is probably Mozart's most original symphony, and the "Jupiter," No. 41, a crowning achievement for him in the medium of the symphony.

It is with the last symphonies of Haydn and Mozart that the eighteenth-century instrumental form reaches its summit. What was said at the beginning of this section on the changing attitude and aspect of this medium in the course of the century is best exemplified in the works of these composers. Their efforts lead directly to Beethoven and a new era in symphonic music. The symphony of the eighteenth century was an amalgamation of many forms and styles ranging from chamber music to opera. The concerto, the divertimento, the operatic aria, all contributed essential features of color and techniques which were to make it such an important genre in the nineteenth century.

Beethoven's first two symphonies, written in 1800 and 1802, respectively, are in the tradition of Haydn or at least the Viennese school. Each is cast in four movements. The third movement of No. 1 in C major, Op. 21, although marked *Menuetto,* already has the fast pace of the scherzo. In Symphony No. 2 in D major, Op. 36, the third movement is marked *Scherzo,* but the style is more akin to the Haydn minuet. Both symphonies commence with a slow introduction. Except for the final movement of No. 2, the first, slow, and last movements are cast in sonata-form. The finale of No. 2 is in that hybrid form seemingly invented by Haydn, the sonata-rondo. There are sharp contrasts in each movement when, for example, a tender theme is interrupted with brusque interjections.

The normal constituency of the orchestra at the time Beethoven wrote these works was 8-14 violins, 2-4 violas, 2-4 cellos, 1-3 basses. If there are 8 violins, the wind instruments are in single pairs; if 12 to 14 violins are used, the winds may be doubled except for the trumpet parts.

Commencing with the "Eroica" Symphony, No. 3 in E-flat major, Op. 55 (1804), a new spirit enters the symphony. Beethoven created in his music a rhythmic propulsion that often drives the music in a headlong dash, as in the first and last movements of his 7th Symphony in A major, Op. 92 (1812), that in an earlier age could not have been tolerated. The sudden, exaggerated moves from *forte* to *piano* and vice versa, wide intervalic leaps, and all manner of bizarre devices are far removed from the noble, poised philosophy of the Classic era. And yet the solid architectonic construction, the methods of developing his material, and his reliance on forms stemming from the eighteenth century place Beethoven in the category of the Classic composer. An examination of first movements shows him to be more concerned with balance than his predecessors. In Symphony No. 4 in B-flat major, Op. 60 (1806), No. 5 in C minor, Op. 67 (1807), and No. 6 in F major, Op. 68 (1808), each of the sections, the exposition, the development, and the recapitulation, is the same length or within one or two measures of being the same length. In the 5th Symphony, perhaps the best known symphony of any ever written, the exposition is 124 measures long, the development 123, and the recapitulation 127. Even the coda, although outside the design proper, is 128 measures in length. With few exceptions Beethoven adheres to the traditional key relationships normally found in sonata-form. In that respect he is far more conservative in the symphonies than he is in his pianoforte sonatas.

As we found in the eighteenth century, the slow movements vary in design. Sonata-form is used in the 4th and 6th along with a sonatina design in the Symphony No. 8 in F major, Op. 93 (1812). The famous Marche funebre in the "Eroica" is cast in song and trio form, A B A'. But in the 5th, 7th, and Symphony No. 9 in D minor, Op. 125 (1824), he resorts to the use of one of his favorites, the theme and variations. Beethoven was a master in the construction of variations. Sometimes the theme and variations are used as an end in themselves, as in the 5th, or sometimes as a means to an end—as a part of a larger design. Thus in the 7th, in song and trio design, the variations occupy the area of the principal song, while contrasting material sets off the trio. In the 9th the slow movement is a rondo design with the variations occupying the principal song areas. When the themes themselves are lyric and expressive, Beethoven does little more than vary the theme by ornamentation or rhythmic modification as in the 5th and 9th. But if the theme is harmonic or chordal in style as in the 7th, it allows him to superimpose melodic ideas over the harmony.

It is in the dance movements that Beethoven displays some of his most original ideas. Commencing with the 3rd Symphony we have a genuine scherzo. Indeed this is the norm for all scherzi in music, the basis for comparison. All others are like this or differ from it. Since the minuet was no longer danced in the ballroom, its inclusion in symphonies of this period would seem anachronistic. Taking its departure from the meter of the minuet, 3-4, the scherzo moves at an extremely rapid pace. In the "Eroica" we also find a reiterated note pattern like the stipple effect in the graphic arts. These then are some of the important characteristics of the scherzo. With respect to design Beethoven stayed within the principles of the song and trio idea. However, instead of indicating in the score that the principal song is to be repeated verbatim as we find in eighteenth-century symphonies, Beethoven wrote out the repetition and made some modifications. In the 3rd Symphony he changed the meter in one part of the codetta in the principal song to duple meter. Such subtle changes also indicate that the public too was weary of hearing exact and obvious repetitions in the dance movement.

While Beethoven stayed with the principle of the A B A design, we note certain exterior and interior expansions of the form. In the 4th Symphony he repeats the trio and part of the principal song to give us an A B A B A design. This is what is meant by exterior expansion. Similarly the 6th and 7th Symphonies carry out this idea. Even more impressive is what Beethoven did in the scherzo movement of the 9th. Here the principal song, normally cast in a simple a b a plan, is a sonata-form complete with exposition, development, and recapitulation. This is interior expansion.

Not all dance movements in his symphonies are indicated as scherzi, although they may contain scherzo characteristics. The 5th Symphony, for example, is simply marked *Allegro*. It moves in rapid 3-4 meter but lacks the scherzo spirit. The character of the opening theme is suave, lyric, and mysterious. The 7th Symphony has all the characteristics of a scherzo but is labeled only *Presto*. Having been criticized for some of his avant-garde compositions, Beethoven, with tongue in cheek, wrote his 8th in the style of the eighteenth-century symphony. For the dance movement he included a minuet. But it is a parody of the old minuet. The composer causes everything to go astray: the timpani fall in what seem to be the wrong beats, and accents are demanded at illogical places.

Like Mozart, Beethoven used the sonata-form in most of his final movements (Symphonies 4 through 7). The 8th Symphony, again in imitation of the Classic period, used the hybrid form associated with Haydn, the sonata-rondo. In the 3rd and 9th Symphonies he utilized the theme and variations principle. The fourth movement of the "Eroica" is one of the great movements in symphonic literature, the aesthetician's ideal. It is indeed a theme and variations, but the plan is worked out to incorporate the sense of a sonata-form. The two-part theme is really not a melody at all but a kind of harmonic outline sounded without accompaniment. Such a theme allows Beethoven to erect lyric melodies over this harmonic outline. One of these lyric themes gradually assumes, in the course of the movement, more importance than the original theme and is used to climax the whole movement. The 9th Symphony, which employs chorus and vocal soloists in addition to the orchestra in the final movement, is also based on a theme and variations.

Of significance in the organization of the symphony as a whole is Beethoven's idea of creating unity throughout the work. This unity may consist of simple repetition of thematic material heard in previous movements and reiterated in subsequent movements or it may go further by altering the character of the thematic material on its repetition, a kind of metamorphosis or transformation. In the final movement of the 9th Symphony Beethoven wrote a lengthy introduction in which he has the main theme of each of the previous three movements sounded in turn, unaltered in style. But in the 5th Symphony, where the "motto" theme of the first movement appears in the third and fourth movements, the repetition is not just one of simple reminiscence as in the 9th, but of transformation. Where the "motto" theme of the first movement was nervous and frenetic, it appears noble or at least dignified in the third. This metamorphosis is created by the manipulation of the elements of music: rhythmic change, meter change, and orchestration.

Beethoven: Symphony No. 5. First Movement, "Motto" Theme

Allegro con brio

Third Movement, "Motto" Theme transformed

Allegro

Later in the movement, on the return of the principal song, the character of this theme is changed even further. Instead of the noble, outgoing theme it seemed to be, it now appears ghostly and mysterious, being sounded *pianissimo* by pizzicato strings instead of *fortissimo* in the horns. At the close of the development section in the fourth movement Beethoven again repeats the ghostly mood of the "motto" theme before plunging back to the triumphant theme of the finale.

Beethoven is the great transitional figure between the Classic and Romantic periods. Steeped as he was in eighteenth-century traditions he nevertheless had such powers of creative energy that went far beyond the smugness of the Classic era. The times were ripe for new ideas. So great was his influence that he served as a model for the whole of the nineteenth century. Every composer seemed to sense Beethoven's image looking over his shoulder. He either stood in awe of the master or was determined to write better.

Supplementary Reading

Einstein. *Mozart: His Character, His Work.* pp. 215-236.
Landon, H. C. Robbins. *The Symphonies of Joseph Haydn.*
This is a comprehensive study of the symphonies which is of inestimable aid in seeking information about any specific work.
Landon & Mitchell. *The Mozart Companion.* pp. 156-199.
Moore, Earl V., and Theodore E. Heger. *The Symphony and the Symphonic Poem.*
For any study of the symphonies of the Classic era the charts in this book serve as ground floor plans to guide the listener through the labyrinth of sound he will experience.

Suggested Listening

The repertory of recorded symphonies is vast. However specific titles are avoided here because shortly after being issued, recordings are frequently withdrawn from the manufacturer's catalog. Almost all of the hundred or more symphonies of Haydn are now available as are all those of Mozart and Beethoven.

Of the earlier works, those of Sammartini, Mīča, Monn, Wagenseil, the composers of the Mannheim school, especially Stamitz, C.P.E. and J.C. Bach should be investigated.

SYMPHONIE CONCERTANTE

Close on the heels of the concerto in popularity in the Classic period was the *symphonie concertante.* This was a work for two or more solo instruments and orchestra in which elements of the solo concerto, the old Baroque *concerto grosso,* the divertimento, and the symphony were fused. As a medium of instrumental music it enjoyed its greatest popularity around 1770. It made a direct appeal to the audiences of the time who enjoyed so much a display of virtuosity and a fondness for big sonority. It was a type which originated in France. It is estimated that during the eighteenth century some 200 such compositions were written by 46 Parisian composers. The accompanying orchestra in the *symphonie concertante* paralleled that of the symphony at that time. The solo group varied from two to six performers. All manner of solo combinations was used. Mozart's are among the most popular performed today. He wrote one for violin, viola, and orchestra, and one for oboe, clarinet, bassoon, horn, and orchestra. The *concertante* which Haydn composed for a London concert included oboe, bassoon, violin, and cello in the solo group. It should be understood that although this medium was of French origin, composers of all countries, especially Germany, indulged in the writing of *concertantes*.

sacred music

Sacred music in the whole of the eighteenth century derived its nourishment from opera. The aria, the recitative, and the instrumental accompaniment which form such a substantial part of music for the church all came from the music drama of the seventeenth and eighteenth centuries. These elements, combined with the choruses of the old German motet, helped to formulate the cantata and oratorio in the Baroque. However it must be realized that sacred music in the eighteenth century no longer held the fascination for composers that it did in previous eras. The agnostic and even atheistic attitudes that prevailed, the waning political influence of the church, and the hard fact that the secular music field was more lucrative for a composer, all led to a general decline of interest in sacred music.

As we have seen in both opera and instrumental music, the styles of sacred music too changed with each generation. The Baroque utilized an elaborate polyphonic setting in a goodly portion of its music, and in the Protestant North the Lutheran chorales formed an integral part of the compositions. In contrast, the sacred works of the Rococo are shallow. One notes immediately that the sincerity of the Baroque is totally lacking. This is due largely to the influence of Georg Philipp Telemann (1681-1767), one of the most significant and prolific composers in the eighteenth century. The church music of the Classic period seems to us too operatic and even flippant, but then the Classic era did not make a sharp distinction between sacred and secular. It believed that anything that is worthy and artistic in secular life is dignified and proper in the church. The optimistic outlook which prevailed in this period is fully expressed in its music. It is noteworthy too that the best sacred music was written not in the Protestant North as in the Baroque but in the Catholic South.

As in opera, the virtuosity of solo singers in the course of the eighteenth century was greatly admired in the church service. The *prima donna* and the *primo uomo* made their appearances in the choir. This was made possible by a Catholic church decree which declared that any musician, whether or not he had clerical status, was eligible for a church position.

Although style changed with each generation, one feature seems common to all choral music in the church, and that is counterpoint. We have spoken of the condemnation of counterpoint in the secular music of the Rococo. The musicians of this generation considered it a basic discipline for students of composition and seemingly, aside from its pedagogical value, as appropriate only for church music. The counterpoint in the Rococo and the Classic periods is nevertheless controlled by a homophonic substructure.

Since the anthems and cantatas prevalent in the Protestant countries in the latter part of the eighteenth century are so insignificant in the light of church music written in Catholic countries, especially by Haydn and Mozart in Austria, it seems reasonable to devote our whole attention to works by these men. In the Catholic service we can expect to find settings for Masses, Psalms, motets, antiphons, hymns, litanies, oratorios, Passions, and sacred songs. Of these the most important in the Rococo and Classical eras is the Mass.

The Neapolitan opera composers in the early eighteenth century dictated the style of the Mass. Practices from the opera, the symphony, and chamber music all mingled in their compositions for liturgical purposes. Antonio Caldara (1670-1736), an Italian composer of 87 operas and some 30 Masses, was engaged as vice-conductor under Fux in Vienna in 1716. His Mass settings may have been influential on Haydn. An important feature of musical settings for the Mass in the eighteenth century was the sectionalization of each movement. The various thoughts expressed in the texts of each portion of the Ordinary of the Mass—Kyrie, Gloria, Credo, Sanctus, Agnus Dei—allowed for musical digressions in tempo, mood, texture, and key dictated by the meaning of the words. This sectionalization had sprung largely from the Italian secular cantata. Thus the Credo might be made divisible into three or four sections (Bach, in his B minor Mass, has eight) utilizing not only chorus but solo voices in arias, duets, and ensembles—all derived from opera.

Settings for the Mass in the Classic period also show the influence of instrumental composition. The solution to the problems of form and style in instrumental music was transformed and assimilated into what eventually became a new style for the Mass. From the symphony came orchestral color and designs like the sonata-form and the rondo. Since composers were especially concerned with the problem of musical form, we find that the spirit of the texts and the music itself correspond only loosely. Because the construction was dictated almost entirely by musical logic, disturbing features in the text—disturbing that is to church authority and rules—often result. Thus in Mozart's Mass in C minor (K.139), where the first part of the Kyrie returns, the words "Kyrie eleison" and "Christe eleison" alternate in a catch-as-catch-can manner. Combining vocal and instrumental techniques in a complex composite of forms and styles is part and parcel of the eighteenth-century Mass.

From the awkward, experimental stages we find at the beginning of the century, the Mass grew to be a thing of beauty, with movements falling into prescribed, standardized schemes. So that when Mozart and Haydn appear on the scene, much of the spade work for what we call the symphonic-polyphonic Mass was completed. All that remained was for these masters to add their touch of genius.

The orchestras used to accompany church music in the Rococo and Classic eras were generally small, with an instrumentation not unlike what one might find in the court orchestras. Strangely enough trombones are frequently a part of the instrumentation. The use of these brass instruments had long been associated with music in the church. Occasionally, for special effects, they might be used in the opera orchestra, but not in symphony orchestras until the last decade of the eighteenth century, and then largely in French ensembles. The function of the orchestra was simply to reinforce the vocal parts, but it was also entrusted with short preludes and interludes.

In 1783 Emperor Joseph II, ruler of the Holy Roman Empire, published an ordinance limiting the use of instrumental forces in church to important festivals. Orchestral music was permitted only in the imperial chapel in Vienna, in the cathedral where the archbishop was officiating, and in other churches only on special feast days. The presence of an orchestra was, according to the emperor, a costly and extravagant luxury. However, such a tyranny could never bring about a musical reform. The decree was lifted in 1791. It is interesting to note that Haydn for one wrote no Masses during this eight-year period of austerity.

Austrian Masses in the eighteenth century were divided into two basic categories: the *Missa brevis*, or Short Mass, and the *Missa Solemnis*, or Solemn (*Missa longa*) Mass. In the *Missa brevis* the proportions of the individual movements as well as the vocal and instrumental resources were limited. For example, the orchestration may consist of little more than two violin parts and bass, the bass being realized by the organ. The Gloria and Credo of the Ordinary of the Mass have rather lengthy texts. So composers always set the texts syllabically, whereas a movement like the Kyrie or Agnus Dei could be set melismatically, with many notes to a single syllable of text. Another method of speeding the movement used by composers was to arrange the text so that several voices sang separate words of the text simultaneously. The words under these circumstances could hardly be intelligible to the congregation. Such a procedure aroused the criticism of the clergy who claimed, and rightly so, that the clarity and meaning of the texts were invariably lost. Karl Georg Reuter (1708-1772), the Kapellmeister of St. Stephen's Cathedral in Vienna and the man who accepted Haydn in the choir as a boy soprano, wrote a Gloria in one of his *Misse brevis* in which four different texts appear simultaneously, one each for the soprano, alto, tenor, and bass parts of the choir.

The *Missa Solemnis*, on the other hand, allows for a full-scale musical treatment. If it were composed for a particular festive occasion, it would undoubtedly include trumpets and timpani and be cast in the key of C major. In the Göttweig Abbey Collection, 70% of the Masses written before 1800 are in C major. This interesting statistic is reflected in the many Masses Mozart wrote in the same key, especially those he wrote for Salzburg. At St. Stephen's in Vienna, trombones were used for the big Masses as well as oboes, bassoons, and horns. Flutes were less often used. When the flute is used, it generally serves as an obbligato instrument in a vocal solo. Clarinets do not appear in scores until after 1790.

With respect to the individual movements, the Kyrie presents us with a good example of a vocal movement derived from an instrumental design. It is frequently cast in sonata-form. This can readily be seen in Haydn's *Missa in Tempore Belli* (Mass in Time of War), better known as the "Paukenmesse," or Drum Mass, and in his *Misse in Augustiis,* or "Lord Nelson Mass."

The Gloria is usually a three-part form. It begins with a quick tempo up to the words "Qui tollis peccate mundi" (Who takest away the sins of the world). From here the second part begins, more likely in a slow tempo. With the phrase "Quoniam tu solus sanctus" (For Thou only art holy) the original lively tempo resumes. The "Amen" which concludes the Gloria is usually a fugal section.

Because of its lengthy text and varied thoughts the Credo appears in at least three or in several sections. The opening of the movement proceeds in a rather rapid tempo with the text set in a straight-forward, syllabic style. A dramatic change in the character of the music commences with the words "Et incarnatus est" (And was incarnate by the Holy Ghost). The tempo slows to an expressive *largo* or *adagio*. The composer will often take this occasion to allow a soloist to sing this portion. At the pronouncement of "Et resurrexit tertia die" (And the third day He rose again), a bright, exultant tempo is instituted. The "Amen" at the close is treated in a similar manner to that of the Gloria.

The Sanctus is cast in a two-part design. It begins in a slow, majestic manner in keeping with the initial sentence. With "Pleni sunt coeli" (The heavens and the earth are full of Thy glory) the tempo speeds up. Then there is a bright close on "Hosanna." The Benedictus, like the Sanctus, is constructed of two sections: the "Benedictus" forms the first part, usually in lyrical style and in a slow tempo; the "Hosanna," the second part, more dramatic and faster in tempo. To provide a modicum of unity, the "Hosanna" of the Benedictus may be set to the same music as the "Hosanna" of the Sanctus.

The final movement of the Mass, the Agnus Dei, has no generalized plan of setting as we find in the foregone movements. Because of the subjective character of the text, composers treat the movement in a very personal way. Sometimes only soloists are used, sometimes the full choir. The tempo may vary from a moderate to a very slow one, and the mode might be major, or it might be minor. But with the words "Dona nobis pacem" (Grant us peace), a sharp change in the spirit of the music takes place. Composers are given to setting this last phrase of the text in fugal style and in a fast tempo.

Mozart wrote approximately sixty works suitable for church services including fifteen Masses and a Requiem Mass (K.626; Mass for the dead), left uncompleted. His experiences in writing in the Italian operatic style, the effect on him of the Storm and Stress movement in Germany, and the expert craftsmanship he had developed in Salzburg all make of his sacred music something very special: a noble, transparent, yet solidly-constructed style. Counterpoint is integrated with the homophonic texture. Among the fifteen Masses which he wrote during his lifetime, the two outstanding ones are those dated 1779 and 1780, respectively. Both are in C major and bear the catalog numbers K.317 and K.337. The one completed on March 23, 1779, has the subtitle "Coronation," so called because it was used for a festival service commemorating the coronation of a miraculous image of the Virgin in the Church of Maria-Plain above Salzburg. Both Masses call for almost identical orchestration in the Salzburg tradition: oboes, bassoons, horns, trumpets, trombones, timpani, and strings *sans* violas. An element of unity is added in the "Coronation" Mass when in the last movement Mozart uses a theme from the Kyrie for the setting of the "Dona nobis pacem."

Perhaps the apex of his settings of the Ordinary of the Mass comes with the work in C minor, K.427, which he wrote during the period of 1782-1783. Unfortunately it was never completed. The Kyrie, an elaborate treatment of the Gloria, the Sanctus, and the Benedictus are there, but he did not compose an Agnus Dei at all, and the Credo exists only in fragments. However, the work was performed during his lifetime at St. Peter's Church in Salzburg in August of 1783. Mozart seems to have composed the elaborate soprano solos contained in the Mass as a vehicle for his wife, Constanze, for she did sing one of the two soprano solo parts in Salzburg at the performance there. Mozart not only used a large orchestra but a large chorus as well, divided not only in the four parts normally found in church music but into five and eight parts. The texture in the choral sections has a thicker polyphonic texture than we find in the previous Masses. This is about the time Mozart made his acquaintance with the works of Bach and Handel and was simply overwhelmed with what he had discovered. The four movements that comprise this Mass are among the greatest in Austrian church music.

One of the last works Mozart composed was a Requiem Mass (K.626), a Mass celebrated for the repose of the souls of the dead. So many rumors surround its history that we probably will never know the authentic details of its composition. Here are a few facts. Count Walsegg, a wealthy nobleman, commissioned a Requiem Mass of Mozart in July of 1791 and gave him a substantial down payment. At the time, Mozart was busy completing work on his operas, *The Magic Flute* and *The Clemency of Titus,* and worked on the Mass sporadically. In the fall of that year Mozart concentrated his attention upon his commission, but he died on December 5 with the Mass incomplete. Only the first movement (*Introitus: Requiem aeternam*) and the Kyrie were completed in their entirety. The balance of the work through the "Hostias et preces" in the Offertorium was sketched out, including the vocal parts and indications for the orchestration. Mozart's widow feared she would have to return the honorarium advanced by Count Walsegg. She approached Joseph Eybler, then court conductor in Vienna, and asked him to complete it. When he refused, she turned to one of Mozart's pupils, Franz

Süssmayer, who undertook to finish the Requiem. Because his manuscript was so much like Mozart's, Constanza was able to pass the completed score on to Count Walsegg as Mozart's own. The deception was not discovered until the nineteenth century, and scholars have tried to decide ever since what was Mozart's and what was Süssmayer's part in the composition. Mozart did succeed in putting down all his intentions in a kind of shorthand which Süssmayer could easily have translated, but there are no sketches for the last three movements. The balance of the Requiem was probably composed by Süssmayer. The deception must have been successful, for even these movements seem to bear the characteristic Mozartean touch.

The orchestration is unusual for Mozart. Of the woodwind family he uses only two bassett horns (a species of clarinet) and two bassoons. No horns are used, but he scores for trumpets, trombones, and timpani as well as strings. Such an orchestration results in a dark, somber-toned timbre.

Again, as we have seen in some of the last Solemn Masses Mozart wrote, there is evoked memories of the past—of Bach and Handel. This is especially true of the Kyrie with its double fugue. But aside from technical matters the Requiem remains one of the sublime expressions and one of the great treasures of our heritage.

Haydn wrote fourteen Masses, one of which is lost. Three belong to the *Missa brevis* category, the balance are *Misse Solemnis* and are among the greatest works of their kind ever composed. The earliest preserved composition of Haydn is his first Mass, a *Missa brevis* in F major, written when he was seventeen, and his last Mass, the *Harmoniemesse,* was written when he was seventy. To his biographer Griesinger he once remarked, "I am rather proud of my Masses," and he had every right to be.

When Werner, the Kapellmeister of the Eszterházy family, died in 1766, Haydn, who replaced him, took over the duties of preparing the music for the services in the Eisenstadt Castle chapel. It was in that year that he wrote his first big Mass, dedicated to the Blessed Virgin Mary. The Mass helped to establish Haydn's reputation, for copies were circulated all over Europe as far away as Spain. When the Emperor issued his decree of 1793 that the instrumental forces were to be limited in music for the church, Haydn wrote no Masses for fourteen years. It is in his adept handling of orchestral forces that much of Haydn's greatest strength lies.

After his famous London sojourns, Haydn returned in 1796 to the active service of Prince Nikolaus II of Eszterházy, the fourth patron of this aristocratic house under which the composer had served for more than thirty years. By this time Haydn's fame had spread throughout Western Europe, and the Prince was wise enough not to dictate to Haydn what the composer should write. Nikolaus, an ardent lover of church music, did make one request, however, and that was to ask Haydn to compose a Mass each year for performance in the Bergkirche in Eisenstadt. During these late years Haydn divided his time between the Eszterházy palace in Eisenstadt and his house in Gumpendorf, then a charming suburb of Vienna but now in the middle of the city. In these two places Haydn began a series of works which propelled him on to even greater heights. This included six Masses which are all on a large scale utilizing orchestra with trumpets and timpani, chorus, and vocal soloists. The symphonic style, already described, affects not only the texture but the form as well. The accompaniment, no longer merely a support for the voices, is often independent of the choral parts. Certain traditional factors are retained including the use of choral fugues at the close of the Gloria and Credo. But the opera-inspired recitative and solo aria have all but disappeared. Instead a quartet of soloists is lifted out of the chorus tutti to create an aura of intimacy which the text often requires.

If one were to choose his favorite among the last six Masses of Haydn, he would be in a position similar to the person attempting to choose his favorite among the last six piano concertos of Mozart. Although the *Misse in Augustiis,* better known as the "Lord Nelson" Mass, has long been among the most popular, especially in Austria, equally great are the *Mass in Time of War,* the *Heiligmesse,* the *Theresienmesse,* and the *Schöpfungsmesse* (Creation Mass). Their steadfast unity of purpose and greatness of expression help to bring to a climax the career of one of our greatest creative artists.

There remain two works in this category by Haydn that should be considered, his oratorios *The Creation* and *The Seasons.* It is strange that Haydn in his last years would turn to a medium such as the oratorio which was at that time all but obsolete. True he had tried his hand at composing an oratorio in the mid-70's, *Il ritorno di Tobias* (The Return of Tobias), which he wrote for a benefit performance for the Viennese Society of Blind Artists. *Il ritorno* imitates the style of the Italian oratorio of the first half of the eighteenth century, and even at that time the style was rather outmoded. But with this single isolated example Haydn wisely abandoned this form as unsuitable. It has extremely difficult solo numbers, excellent choruses, and a brilliant orchestration.

One fact, it is necessary to realize in the history of music, is that until the nineteenth century no one was interested in music of the past.

This is hard for us in the twentieth century to contemplate because we have made such a fetish of reviving music even of ancient vintage. Not only do we perform the music but we try to revive it with authentic instruments and according to the tuning concepts of that time. Suppose though that we were to listen, as they did through history, only to contemporary music—no more Bach or Beethoven, no more Brahms or Mozart. A composer wrote his music to order and generally for a special occasion. Perhaps his piece would have one performance and then be discarded without it ever being heard again. Even operas seldom survived the season for which they were written. One strange exception occurred in England. There in the eighteenth century Handel's oratorios, especially *Messiah,* continued to be performed by various choral organizations after the composer's death in 1759. When Haydn visited London in 1791, he had occasion to hear a performance of *Messiah* in Westminster Abbey. The "Halleluja Chorus" moved him to tears, and he is said to have exclaimed of Handel, "He is the master of us all." But more important was Haydn's reflection that perhaps it is possible that a composer's music might live after him. At least a more idealistic attitude seems to have been taken by him. There is no doubt that from this time on Handel influenced Haydn's treatment of choral writing in his Masses and oratorios.

When Haydn returned from London in 1795, he brought with him a libretto in English based on the biblical story of the Creation and on Milton's *Paradise Lost.* The libretto had been handed to him by Salomon. Haydn submitted the libretto to the Baron Gottfried van Swieten (1734-1803), a musical amateur of great importance in Vienna, for translation and adaptation into German. Born of an aristocratic family and holding responsible diplomatic and civil posts, Van Swieten assumed the air of a musical autocrat. The author of the original English text is to date unknown, and the copy of the libretto which Salomon gave to Haydn is lost. Likewise Haydn's autograph score of *The Creation* (*Die Schöpfung*) disappeared in 1803, together with that of *The Seasons.* Only Van Swieten's autograph German text is extant, a valuable document for the detailed musical instruction which Van Swieten noted in the margins. From his own admission Van Sweiten handled the English text quite freely. Typical of German writers of the period, the libretto is sentimental and saccharine. Nevertheless it must have been inspiring to Haydn, for *The Creation* is one of the composer's greatest works.

Haydn adopted the curious arrangement of the seventeenth-century Italian oratorio in which the story is recited by several narrators, here the three archangels, Gabriel, Uriel, and Raphael. The six days of creation are unfolded in a series of pictures and words of thanks and

praise addressed to the Creator. The end of each working day is celebrated with hymns by the choirs of heavenly hosts. Haydn aimed to
make the orchestra and chorus the pillars of his structure with the
space between reserved for arias and the accompanied recitatives. As
in his Masses, Haydn combined one or more solo voices with the chorus
and orchestra. The overture is one of the most impressive pieces Haydn
ever wrote and in places seems to anticipate Wagner. Only an experienced composer of symphonies could realize the expressiveness Haydn
achieves here and in the orchestral interludes and accompaniment. *The
Creation* had its first performance on April 29, 1798.

The text of *The Seasons* (*Die Jahreszeiten*) was derived from James
Thompson's (1700-1748) verses of the same title which had been published in England between 1726 and 1730. Again the Baron van Swieten
was approached to provide a suitable libretto drawn from Thompson's
poem, and like his adaptation and translation of the text for *The
Creation,* it is a travesty of Thompson's work. But the success of
the oratorio is due to the marvelous and sometimes naïve way Haydn
depicts nature and the innocence of man in a pastoral setting. As in
The Creation there are magnificent choruses and stunning arias as well
as striking writing for the orchestra. Both these oratorios serve as a
fitting climax to the career of one of the most respected composers in
the history of music.

Beethoven wrote two Masses, one in C major, Opus 86, and the
great Missa Solemnis in D major, Opus 123. The order for the first
came from Prince Eszterházy in 1807, and because Eszterházy's tastes
were conservative and because Haydn, although retired, was still the
nominal head of the musical establishment at Eszterháza, Beethoven was
at first hesitant about accepting the commission. On completing the
Mass he wrote to the Prince as follows: "May I say that I will turn
over the Mass to you with much misgiving as you are used to having
the inimitable masterpieces of the great Haydn performed for you."

Beethoven was religious, believing in a supreme being, but he was
not an ecclesiastic. Being ignorant of Latin he insisted that a literal
German translation of the text of the Ordinary of the Mass be prepared
for him so that he could match the music with the emotional feeling
evoked by the words. He wrote the Mass for four solo voices, a mixed
chorus, and an orchestral accompaniment. There are no solo arias, and
the quartet of solo voices is used only to effect contrast with the chorus.
There is none of the theatricality generally associated with the Masses
of Haydn and Mozart, and it is liturgically practical.

The composer himself conducted the first performance on September
13, 1807, at the Eszterházy castle in Eisenstadt. The Prince was not

too pleased, and Beethoven, quite disgruntled, left the same day for his home in Vienna. The Mass seemed too revolutionary in style for his day and is too conservative for our tastes today.

The five movements of the C minor Mass are treated much like that described earlier. Beethoven cast the Kyrie in a three-part design, an A B A' plan, the Gloria in three sections with changes of tempo at the appropriate changes in the contents of the text, the Credo in four sections with a typical close using a fugue. Beethoven divided the Sanctus into four sections, including the Benedictus, and the final "Hosanna" he made a fugue. The Agnus Dei appears in three sections, and at the very end, on the words "Dona nobis pacem," the composer returns to the theme of the opening Kyrie, thus creating a musical unity for the Mass.

In 1818 Beethoven heard that the Archduke Rudolph was to be made Archbishop of Olmütz. He set about to compose a Mass with a view to having it performed at the installation ceremony. Two years later, when the ceremony took place, the Mass was still incomplete. Not until 1823 did Beethoven finish the Missa Solemnis in D major. As a matter of fact he never lived to hear the work performed in its entirety. Only the Kyrie, Credo, and Agnus Dei were presented on a concert program along with the premiere of the Symphony No. 9 at the Kärtnerthor-Theater in Vienna on May 7, 1824. Like Bach's Mass in B minor it is completely impractical for liturgical purposes. The length of the work and the subsequent duration of the individual sections would make an ecclesiastical ceremony, for which the Mass was intended, almost an irreverent interruption.

It is a typical symphonic-polyphonic Mass of the time held together by recurring motives and thematic development. In that respect it resembles a five-movement symphony. Despite the awe with which conductors have approached the work, it has never been too popular with audiences. First of all Beethoven was completely unsympathetic in his treatment of the human voice. Such unvocal things as the use of a high *tessitura*, lengthy phrases, and the percussive articulation of the melodic-rhythmic patterns only confirm what Beethoven himself said: "When I think of a theme, it is always for some instrument." However Beethoven considered it the best thing he had ever written, which only confirms the dictum that composers are notoriously unreliable judges of their own output.

For the accompaniment Beethoven used a large orchestra: Full woodwinds in pairs, 4 horns, 2 trumpets, 3 trombones, timpani, strings, and the organ. Like the Mass in C major he also used a quartet of soloists along with the chorus.

The Kyrie is again in a three-part design with the "Christe eleison" in a slower tempo and in a minor key. The Gloria is written in six contrasting sections but welded into a single movement. Like the C major Mass there are alternations of solo voices with the chorus throughout, fugues, and at the end he returns with the theme of the opening on a repetition of the words "Gloria in Excelsis Deo." The lengthy Credo is unified by repetition of a four-note motive sung by the basses at the outset, "Credo, credo." Some of the seven sections which go to make up the movement are treated with greater importance than others. The "Et incarnatus est" (Adagio), cast in the Dorian mode of ancient times, the "Crucifixus" with its harsh stabbing dissonances in the orchestra, and the great double fugue which closes the movement are among the outstanding sections. In a mood of quiet devotion the Sanctus begins with the quartet of soloists to the accompaniment of trombone chords and low strings. An abrupt change comes with the "Pleni sunt coeli" and the following "Hosanna," both treated in a fugal manner. There is a *Praeludium* for orchestra alone which is to serve as background music for the most dramatic moment of the Catholic Mass, the Elevation of the Host. A descending passage for solo violin connects this to the Benedictus set in a kind of pastorale rhythm for chorus.

The whole of the Agnus Dei appears in a minor key and sets a tone of humility and contrition that should move the most hard-hearted music critic. Beethoven inscribed on the score, "Bitte um innern und äussern Frieden" (Prayer for inward and outward peace). The quiet opening is followed by a lively fugato. There are even suggestions of martial music with trumpets and timpani representative of warfare and strife. To this the soloists respond in anguished recitatives on the text "Agnus Dei. . . ." Tension mounts and is broken by a turbulent orchestral Presto. The chorus cries out its "Agnus Dei" again, we have a return of thematic material heard earlier, and the work closes with a triumphant orchestral epilogue.

One senses throughout the Mass that Beethoven had in mind to write a work that was to be used for a particular service of exceptional pomp and magnificence. He used all the resources available to him in the first quarter of the nineteenth century—the symphony orchestra, vocal soloists, and chorus. His skill, his sincerity, his beliefs are all expressed.

Supplementary Reading

Einstein. *Mozart: His Character, His Works.* pp. 319-354.
Landon & Mitchell. *The Mozart Companion.* pp. 361-376.

Láng. *Music in Western Civilization.* pp. 700-708.
Ulrich & Pisk. *A History of Music and Musical Style.* pp. 360-377.

SUGGESTED LISTENING

Of Haydn's twelve Masses, the listener will find the last six to be truly great works, especially No. 7 in C major, the Mass in time of War ("Pauken-messe"), and No. 9 in D minor, Missa in Augustiis, known as the "Lord Nelson Mass." And no one who has not heard them should pass up an opportunity to listen to the two great oratorios, *The Creation* and *The Seasons.*

Mozart's "Coronation" Mass (K.317) and, of course, the famous Requiem Mass (K.626) should be in the listening repertory of every music lover.

the musician
in the
eighteenth century

What kind of person was the musician in the period of the Rococo and Classic periods? What were his aspirations, and how far could he go to achieve his ambitions? As we view the sociological conditions of the eighteenth century, we discover that in his own time and environment he was not much different from the musician of today. He was concerned with earning a living, and to do this he had to please his patrons or the public. Compared to the twentieth-century musician he was expected to be far more versatile in his art. He had to be able to perform on an instrument, compose music, and direct concerts, unless, of course, he was a singer. Far less was expected of the vocalist, especially Italian vocalists. The man who specialized as a virtuoso on an instrument wrote and played his own solos, carrying about with him on tour a sheaf of his own sonatas and concertos. It should be understood that through most of the eighteenth century the caste system still prevailed. The musician was largely viewed as a servant. If he were attached to a court, he formed part of the household and wore livery. The traveling virtuoso was considered a mere entertainer with a status no greater than the trouper in the days of vaudeville.

When a child showed aptitude in music and decided to pursue music as a career, he was sent to a conservatory. The conservatory was the unique establishment of Italy, which country held a monopoly on music education in the eighteenth century. Music was one commodity which Italy, then a poor country in natural resources, had to export. Throughout Europe Italian musicians held the key positions in opera houses and orchestras. The great demand everywhere for singers, composers, and instrumentalists was answered by the conservatories. The most famous of these were located in Venice and Naples. The Venetian conservatories (*Scuole*) were originally charitable hospitals for the poor and infirm, built and endowed by private citizens in the Renaissance period. Some were also orphanages or poor houses for children. Starting as educational institutions for the children, they soon began to teach music, which became in time the chief subject. The conservatories were boarding schools operated by the clergy. The Jesuits founded many of these conservatories all over Europe, but on a smaller scale than Venice and Naples. Instruction was free to those whom the faculty deemed sufficiently talented. The instruction was of exceptionally high caliber, and the normal length of training was eight years.

But what about the student who couldn't go to Italy to learn his craft? In the Protestant North he could enter a choir school and there learn some of the fundamentals of his art. More likely, however, he would seek out a private teacher, learn to play his instrument and to compose much as an apprentice learned his craft from a guildmaster.

Now the prospective musician has acquired his training and seeks a position. What opportunities were open to him? First of all there was the court opera. The opera house with its elaborate stage machinery paid exorbitant salaries to obtain the services of the best singers. Only a court could afford the expense involved in supporting an institution devoted to the performance of opera. To sponsor a glamorous opera house increased the court's prestige. The audience was made up of members of the court and guests among the nobility. Many petty courts could not afford the luxury of a permanent opera establishment. The demand of the nobility for opera was met by the traveling opera company organized on a professional level and offering its services on a subscription basis. In some cities there were public opera houses. These commercial opera companies were run by a manager. The nobility and the wealthy merchants were shareholders who subscribed for the boxes. The balance of the seats was sold to the public. These public opera houses became financial speculations often extremely profitable and often ruinous. Perhaps the most successful of these commerical enterprises was San Carlo in Naples which had an eighty-piece orchestra. Since the audience expected new operas each year, operas were performed for only one season and generally only in one house. This accounts for the extraordinarily large number of operas written in the eighteenth century. It is significant to note that houses producing comic operas were never connected with a court. From the beginning they were organized on a commercial basis. Comic opera has always been supported by the upper middle class and the nobility on the basis of subscription. The repertoire of traveling opera companies frequently included comic operas, for this type involved less expensive stage settings and fewer characters.

In the early eighteenth century public concerts were practically non-existent. Musical life was privately organized, largely by the nobility and the clergy. Most noblemen maintained a private orchestra in their courts. But what of the upper middle class? How were its wants fulfilled? True, the churches frequently offered concerts on a semi-public basis. Church musicians were usually paid from municipal funds. But the middle class too had its musical organizations. In the larger cities amateur orchestras and ensembles were formed, mostly on a private basis. The two main types were (1) the *collegium musicum,* consisting largely of university students, and (2) music clubs or *consorts* (ensembles) of wealthy amateurs. These groups met regularly for practice and concerts. However, only members and their invited guests were admitted. If our young musician set out on a career as a traveling virtuoso, he had to make contact with these groups in order to be heard and to further his career. An audience as we know it today was non-existent.

Concerts at which individual artists and traveling virtuosi performed were called academies. These academies, originally scholarly and artistic societies, became important centers of musical life. At first the concerts presented by the academies were private affairs organized by music societies or clubs whose audiences were made up of wealthy music lovers. Early in the eighteenth century they became commercialized. However, the artist appearing at an academy received little remuneration for his performances. If the artist was dissatisfied with this situation, he could arrange a public concert at his own risk and expense. His remuneration came from subscriptions and the sale of tickets to the public. Commercial academies could already be found in London in the late seventeenth century. This system of public and private academies spread throughout Europe and dominated the concert life of the eighteenth century until the advent of the modern concert manager. Haydn, Mozart, and Beethoven at sometime in their lives performed their works at academy concerts. Beethoven complained bitterly at the meager profit he received. Academies held for charitable purposes appeared under the name of "Benefit Concerts."

The music societies' and the academies' efforts hardly satisfied the demand of a growing middle class for more music. A new method had to be found whereby a greater number of people could be served. This led to the establishment of the concert hall. By combining subscriptions purchased by both the nobility and the upper middle class, it was possible to arrange a "concert season," much as we have today. The basis of the concert season was the establishment of an orchestra which could perform in and fill the hall with sound. The first public concerts on a large scale then were orchestra concerts. In contrast to the *collegium musicum* and the music club made up of amateur musicians, the concert orchestra consisted largely of professionals. This is a new opportunity for our musician seeking employment. These concerts were truly public, for they were open to anyone who subscribed or paid the price of admission.

The first famous orchestra concerts maintained on a commercial basis were the *Concerts Spirituels* in Paris. This great musical institution was founded by Anne-Danican Philidor (1681-1728) in 1725. Philidor, noting that the opera house in Paris was forced to close during the celebration of religious festivals, especially during Lent, proposed to the authorities that concerts be presented on those occasions when the house was closed to performances of opera. Philidor signed a contract with Francine, the impresario of the Opéra, in which he pledged himself to pay 1000 francs a year and to organize public concerts at which both sacred and secular music would be performed. Some twenty-four concerts in all were presented each year. Just before his death in 1728 Philidor transfered his privilege to other managers, and the concerts continued in Paris until political upheavals brought them to a close in 1791. It is at these *Concerts Spirituels* that the French public first heard the symphonies of composers of the Mannheim school and those of Haydn and Mozart as well.

Although public concerts of a limited type had been presented in various ale houses of London as early as the last of the seventeenth century, it was not until Johann Christian Bach and Karl Friedrich Abel (1725-1787), a pupil of J.S. Bach who had migrated to England, collaborated as impresarios that we have the public concerts of which we have been speaking. On February 20, 1764, at Spring Gardens, they presented their first in a series of concerts. These were continued at Almack's and later at the Hanover Square Rooms for seventeen years. Bach's and Abel's efforts were followed by the Professional Concerts which ran from 1783 until 1793. It was at these concerts that the London public was introduced to the symphonies of Haydn and Mozart. But competition with the famous Salomon Concerts, founded in 1791 and for whom Haydn wrote some of his best symphonies, put the Professional Concerts out of business. Johann Peter Salomon (1745-1815) was a

German by birth and English by adoption. Appearing as violin soloist, quartet player (violin and viola), and conductor with the Professional Concerts, he quarreled with the directors and took an independent route. It was by obtaining the personal appearances of Haydn in London and commissioning the composer to prepare symphonies exclusively for his concerts that Salomon's reputation in England was made.

Public concerts were likewise founded in Germany. As early as 1722 Telemann founded public concerts in Hamburg. And although these antedate the *Concerts Spirituels,* they in no way compare to the latter. In Dresden Johann Adam Hiller (1728-1804) devoted himself to promoting the Subscription Concerts in 1763 which eventually developed into the famous Gewandhaus Concerts of which he was appointed conductor. The Gewandhaus Concerts were so called because they were given in the Cloth House.

The public concert was the main form of democratic consumption of music. As the audiences became larger, so did the auditoriums, and as the concert halls grew in size, so did the orchestras needed to fill them with sound. The orchestra was the very backbone of the public concert.

Suppose that our young musician has aspirations to be a composer. To make a name for himself and thus obtain a permanent position, he usually started out by writing a "dedication piece" to a prospective employer. He paid for the engraving from his own pocket and presented the music to this prospective employer in the expectation that he would be remunerated in some way, hopefully more than with the gift of a snuffbox. We will now assume that our musician has been fortunate enough to gain a position as a court composer at a fixed salary. One of the first duties of the employed composer was to write whatever his patron demanded. And the music was written for a specific group of musicians also employed by the court. Since most courts had a limited library of printed music available to them, it was up to the Kapellmeister (our young composer) to keep the musical forces supplied with new music. This is why we are often astounded at the large number of pieces attributed to composers of the eighteenth century. But one thing of which he could be sure, and that was that his music would be performed.

The music composed for the court became the property of that court. Publication of his music was of minor interest to the composer, for most of it was never printed. The composer was unprotected by anything like a copyright law. The only way he could keep anyone else from exploiting his work would be to make sure a copyist or a publisher did not get hold of the music. If a publisher did succeed in obtaining a copy, he could print it and sell it, and the composer had no recourse to law. However a composer could sell his pieces to a publisher for a cash settlement. The composer could then turn around and offer the same pieces to another publisher. Oftentimes, to protect himself, a composer would have his music engraved and published at his own expense, selling copies to the public, unashamedly, at his own house. But there was nothing to prevent the engraver from running off extra copies and selling the composer's music at his own shop.

Operas written for festive occasions at court were sometimes engraved in full score at the expense of the court. This was especially true in France. On the other hand, operas written for commercial companies by staff composers or by commission rarely appeared in print. Since an opera seldom survived longer than the season for which it was written, it was impractical to print a score of the work. Parts were copied by hand. The music copyist was an important employee of the opera house as well as the court. He frequently made considerable extra money by undercover sale of copies. He might copy out the most popular arias of a particular opera and offer them to a publisher who would in turn print and sell them. Thus the copyist might make more money from his transactions than the composer himself.

If our aspiring composer wanted to be free of a position at court or the church, could he, as a free lance composer, make a living? To be sure the commercial opera company such as existed in Venice, Naples, London, and Hamburg, to name a few, and the public concert hall had introduced the free market system into the music business. The composer who wrote for this free market made every attempt to satisfy a demand for which he was uncertain. Under the patronage system he was in close contact with his employer and knew his tastes. He composed when ordered. In the concert hall the audience was anonymous, and the only means the composer had of knowing the reaction of the audience was the amount of applause the music elicited. A spokesman for the anonymous audience was needed now whose business it was to formulate public opinion. Thus was born the music critic or journalist. His first appearance coincides with the beginning of the public concert hall.

What was the free lance composer paid for his music? At the Paris Opera in the 1780's he was paid about $125 for each of the first ten performances of his opera and $70 for each of the next twenty. After that he received no more remuneration. A set of six symphonies or six quartets might sell for about $200. While the free market system quickly conquered and dominated the previous forms of music consumption, particularly after the French Revolution when so many courts abandoned their musical establishments, the composer was left in a more uncertain position. The court composer of opera and orchestral music wrote to supply a specific demand. Composing was part of his contract. The church composer, usually engaged by a municipal administration, also composed under contract.

The free lance composer depended on commissions. Commercial opera companies generally commissioned operas from famous composers. Commercial concert societies like the *Concerts Spirituels,* the Bach-Abel, or Salomon concerts commissioned symphonies from men like Stamitz, Haydn, and Mozart. Salomon paid Haydn about $100 each for the London symphonies.

Under a benevolent patronage system there were three ways music was produced in the eighteenth century: (1) by court order under contract; (2) dedication; (3) commission. From the standpoint of quality there seems to be no difference that can be ascertained between works ordered, dedicated, or commissioned. The composer was at liberty to compose in any style he wished. Most of Mozart's operas were composed by court order. *Don Giovanni* and *The Magic Flute,* however, were commercial commissions. *Figaro,* on the other hand, was written as a free commodity with the hope of a prospective performance in Vienna. Even Beethoven lived in the shadow of the patronage system. Most of his symphonies were still dedication pieces, and his last quartets were commissioned. The Austrian nobility granted him a life annuity because he threatened to accept an offer to become court composer to Napoleon's brother. No composer in the eighteenth century thought it demeaning to accept an order or a commission. Not until the Romantic period did the idea gain ground that music was a free commodity and that if the composer wrote to order, he would lose caste.

When the patronage system declined and democratic music organizations rose, the commissioning system became obsolete. But with the rise of free enterprise along with democratic organizations came a decline in the quantity of music produced. No longer do we have an Alessandro Scarlatti who turned out about 4000 works or a Telemann who turned out even more. It was not uncommon for composers of the Mannheim school to compose a hundred symphonies. Compare these numbers to the amount written by nineteenth- or twentieth-century composers. Indeed the danger of underproduction was averted only because a shift of emphasis in taste resulted in a liking for older instead of contemporary music. The mania for new music under the patronage system gave way to a conservatism under democratic concert life in which contemporary music played a secondary role.

The state too began to assume the role of patron. From the time of the Revolution the French government placed the former court opera under public management and in 1795 founded a national conservatory. The state in other countries commissioned orchestral music and operas.

As we look back on the eighteenth century, we realize that the musician was not much different from the musician in any other period of music history including our own. He strove to make money and to achieve some favor while he lived. And he worked for his own good, not for the approval of posterity. The bulk of the music he wrote served its purpose, and most of it passed into oblivion. But those masterpieces which survived and were accepted by succeeding generations as great works of art have made our stay on earth a little more pleasant.

SUPPLEMENTARY READING

Láng. *Music in Western Civilization.* pp. 708-733.

bibliography

Carse, Adam. *The Orchestra in the XVIIIth Century* (Cambridge: W. Heffer & Sons, 1940).

Einstein, Alfred. *Gluck*. (N.Y.: E.P. Dutton & Co., 1936).

—————. *Mozart: His Character, His Work* (N.Y.: Oxford University Press, 1945).

Geiringer, Karl. *Haydn: A Creative Life in Music*. Rev. ed. (Berkeley: University of California Press, 1968).

Grout, Donald Jay. *A History of Western Music* (N.Y.: W. W. Norton & Co., 1960).

—————. *A Short History of Opera*. 2nd ed. (N.Y.: Columbia University Press, 1965). 2 vols.

Landon, H. C. Robbins. *The Symphonies of Joseph Haydn* (London: Universal Edition & Rockliff, 1955).

Landon, H. C. Robbins, and Donald Mitchell, eds. *The Mozart Companion* (London: Rockliff, 1956).

Láng, Paul Henry. *Music in Western Civilization* (N.Y.: W. W. Norton & Co., 1941).

Moore, Earl V., and Theodore E. Heger. *The Symphony and the Symphonic Poem*. Analytical and Descriptive Charts of the Standard Symphonic Repertory. 5th ed. (Ann Arbor: Ulrich's Books, 1966)

Newman, William S. *The Sonata in the Classic Era* (Chapel Hill: University of North Carolina Press, 1963).

Strunk, Oliver. *Source Readings in Music History* (N.Y.: W. W. Norton & Co., 1950).

Thayer's Life of Beethoven. Rev. & ed. by Elliot Forbes (Princeton, N.J.: Princeton University Press, 1964). 2 vols.

Ulrich, Homer, and Paul A. Pisk. *A History of Music and Musical Style* (N.Y.: Harcourt, Brace, & World, 1963).

index